D1004196

Books by Garry Radison

Poetry

Eye of A Stranger

White Noise

Jeffers' Skull

Non-fiction

Last Words of the Civil War

Last Words: Dying in the Old West

LAST WORDS

OF

THE CIVIL WAR

THE MOMENT OF SACRIFICE

GARRY RADISON

SMOKE RIDGE BOOKS

Canadian Cataloguing in Publication Data

Radison, Garry, 1949-
Last words of the civil war :

Includes bibliographical references and index.
ISBN 0-9688329-1-1 (pbk.)

1. United States--History--Civil War, 1861-1865--Anecdotes.

2. United States--History--Civil War, 1861-1865--Quotations, maxims, etc.

3. Last words.

I. Title.

E468.9.R32 2001 973.7 C2001-910287-9

Cover painting and illustrations by Rita Swanson
Printed and bound in Canada

First Edition

Smoke Ridge Books
P. O. Box 715
Yorkton, SK S3N 2W8
www.smoke-ridge-books.com

For Damon

Acknowledgments

My thanks to the Virginia Institute Archives, J. Kent Langhorne Papers, for the J. Kent Langhorne letter; the Vermont Historical Society for the Elijah Brown letter; The Rare Books and Manuscripts Library of the Ohio State University Libraries for the Rufus Ricksecker letter; The Henry Buckland Local History Miscellaneous Manuscripts Collection, Rutherford B. Hayes Presidential Center, Spiegel Grove, Fremont, Ohio for the Chester Buckland letter; Laverne Ladd Papworth, Rochester Hills, Michigan, for Asa Ladd's letter to his father, and Misty Ladd Flannigan, Dahlgren, Illinois, and her website *The Ladd Digging Ground,* http://homepages.rootsweb.com/~ladd/, for Asa Ladd's letter to his wife; the Eleanor S. Brockenbrough Library, The Museum of the Confederacy, Richmond, for the J. R. Montgomery letter; Thomas Hayes for his informative and entertaining website, *Letters of the Civil War,* http://www.geocities.com/Pentagon/7914/; Al Dalton at the Heritage Preservation Association, Blairs, VA, for finding a copy of the last proclamation of the Confederacy; Kerry Webb for research information; The Sons of Union Veterans of the Civil War for providing the photograph of Albert Woolson; artist Rita Swanson of Churchbridge, SK for her interest and contribution to this project.

The Frederick Pettit letter is contained in The Frederick Pettit Collection of Civil War Letters, (*Civil War Times Illustrated* collection) at the United States Army Military History Institute, Carlisle Barracks, Pennsylvania.

The Robert J. Simmons letter is from *A Grand Army of Black Men.* By Edwin S. Redkey and is reprinted with the permission of Cambridge University Press.

The excerpt from *Frederic Augustus James's Civil War Diary* edited by Jefferson J. Hammer, 1973 is reprinted with the permission of Fairleigh Dickinson University Press.

The material on Edmund Ruffin is reprinted by permission of Louisiana State University Press from *The Diary of Edmund Ruffin, Volume III, A Dream Shattered, June, 1863-June, 1865,* edited by William Kauffman Scarborough. Copyright © 1989 by Louisiana State University Press.

Thanks, also, to the staffs of the Parkland Regional Library, Yorkton, and the Yorkton Public Library for their efforts in obtaining research material.

CONTENTS

LAST WORDS

OF

THE CIVIL WAR

THE MOMENT OF SACRIFICE

INTRODUCTION

The American Civil War was a war of words as much as a war of physical conflict. The politicians and intellectuals argued over definitions of rights of the individual and the state. Common soldiers, a good many of them educated to know "their letters", recorded their experiences in letters and diaries. The new mass media of the time, the newspaper, reported every facet of the war. Modern historians carry on the struggle in the pages of the hundreds of books about the Civil War published each year.

What did the words mean? Abolishment of slavery. Union. States' Rights. Few wars in history have been fought for such noble ideas. On the battlefield, as Stephen Crane astutely surmised, it was a war of courage. More than most wars, it was a war of sacrifice.

The phrase "Famous Last Words" has always caught our attention. In many cases, the last words became "famous" because of the humor or irony they contained. Imagine the crowds watching the regular hangings at, say, Tyburn Crossing on the outskirts of London. A lively, party-going crowd, these observers of death were out for a good time despite the despair of the main participants, out to be entertained by the kicking, struggling, and *last words* of the condemned. And some of those condemned, despite their predicament, enjoyed the attention of the crowd and, putting on a brave front, made an attempt at immortality by uttering Last Words that the crowd might remember and repeat wherever good fellows gathered.

Last Words were also recorded throughout the centuries by priests, especially when they presided at the deathbeds of the more important of their brethren. In church circles, these words would become "famous", studied perhaps by young clerics who, in time, would have to deal with the mysteries of death.

Prayer, blasphemy, bravado, wistful regret—the words were spoken in pain, resignation, acceptance, sometimes relief and, in rare instances, with something akin to euphoria. The language of death, sometimes formal, sometimes, deliberately casual, sometimes foolish, sometimes, perhaps, even noble, is a language we speak with our entire bodies, a moral language that reveals its strength in the determination to proceed even into the dark, to do battle.

The Last Words of the Civil War are not famous; indeed, most of them are obscure. Neither are they particularly witty or humorous. Rather, they express a whole range of human emotions. As well as the expected fear, despair and resignation, there is also courage, hope, pride, compassion, pity, sacrifice, honor—the "old verities and truths of the heart", as William Faulkner said.

These are the last words of individuals who participated in the great event of their time. In the face of death they often responded to the expectations of their peers, dying with brave words on their lips. If accompanied by a chaplain or a female nurse, they often spoke of religion. Warren B. Armstrong explains, "[I]t is important to remember that religion in America at the time of the Civil War had not yet felt the full impact of Darwin's *Origin of Species*...the belief in a life beyond this one with accompanying punishment or reward was more common and much stronger that is the case today." (*For Courageous Fighting and Confident Dying.*)

Many of them spoke of Mother and family in their dying moments, understandable sentiments when one realizes that the men fighting the war were young, sixteen to twenty-five, some even younger. For the most part, they were from the farms and small communities of rural America. Until the war, their opportunities to test themselves as men were limited. Jenkin Lloyd Jones says in his preface to *An Artilleryman's Diary,* "I was a 'mother's boy', and with the exception of three months' schooling at an aunt's house in Watertown, when a little lad, had never been away from home over night."

Young as they were, they had expectations of themselves. Soldier William Stillwell wrote in a letter to his wife, "I expect to try to die like a brave man fighting for the rights of his country and try to die the death of the righteous." One company of soldiers patriotically signed a letter to a newspaper: "Yours till death-for the flag under which we serve." In their final moments, many of these men were concerned more with their courage than with their dying.

The last words of thousands of Confederate soldiers was not a word at all, but the Rebel Yell, a "wild weird falsetto", as historian Bruce Catton described it. Private Arthur van Lisle attempted to set it on paper as, "Hey—Yeh—Yeh! Hey—Yeh—Yeh!" Others have tried to describe it as a high-pitched "Who-who-ey" or "Yai, yai, yi, yai, yi!" The man who died with this yell in his throat was, nonetheless, speaking with the same courage and defiance that artilleryman Mark Kerns articulated at Second Bull Run.

The validity of the last words is an open question. Most quotations were recorded by people who were in attendance or who were near enough to receive them by accurate report. But the reader should retain some skepticism. Under the dramatic and confusing conditions of war, last words were remembered differently by various individuals, all of whom were near the dying man. Many memoirs were written long after the war when memory was not reliable or when the writer was as much interested in telling a good story as in telling the truth. The quotations from author Mary Livermore are particularly suspect, her book containing long quotations written twenty years after the war.

Also evident from the records is a type of selection process. It cannot be merely chance that the last words, mainly of officers, recorded in the official war records are invariably in a patriotic tone and style. Obviously, last words expressing other sentiments were not considered noteworthy by the reporting officers. A similar selection process can by found in the records of chaplains who made lengthy notes of religious last words.

From time to time some zealous storyteller attempted to improve on mundane reality by inventing last words for his subject. One can imagine the old veterans at the reunions telling and re-telling stories of fallen comrades and, in the telling, re-shaping the last words for a more dramatic or humorous tale. The widely reported last words of Stonewall Jackson set the style and mode for dying officers. After the war, biographers and widows often attempted to create similar endings complete with the final noble phrase that would elevate their dead heroes to their rightful places in the great conflict. Some of these fictions have been discredited; others probably remain in the record.

In his *Memoirs of a Volunteer* (W. W. Norton & Company, 1946), Civil War soldier John Beatty relates the following story:

> "An Indiana newspaper reached camp today containing an obituary notice of a lieutenant of the Eighty-eighth Indiana. It gives quite a lengthy biographical sketch of the deceased, and closes with a letter that purports to have been written on the battlefield by one Lieutenant John Thomas, in which Lieutenant Wildman, the subject of the sketch, is said to have been shot near Murfreesboro, and that his last words were, 'Bury me where I have fallen, and do not allow my body to be removed.' The letter is exceedingly complimentary to the said lamented young man, and affirms that 'he was the hero of heroes, noted for his reckless daring, and universally beloved.' The singular feature about the whole matter is that the letter was written by the lamented young officer himself to his own uncle. The deceased justifies his action saying that he had expended two dollars for foolscap and one dollar for postage stamps in writing to the d___d old fool, and never received a reply, and he concluded finally he would write a letter that would interest him."

Lieutenant Wildman's "last words", though pure fiction, are almost identical to the "authentic" last words of many other soldiers. One wonders if the soldiers, sitting by the campfire or lying quietly in their tents on the eve of battle, toyed with various versions of their "last words", re-phrasing them until they caught the right tone, the perfect sentiment and then memorized them for use at the appropriate final moment of their personal stories.

Whatever the method of their creation, last words were actively sought. George F. Linderman writes in *Embattled Courage:* "...those at home hoped desperately for last words that would confirm that their soldier had preserved his decency.... They cherished worthy last words as a special remembrance, as a moral summation of the life about to be lost and as a declaration of religious faith.... On Virginia battlefields the medical attendant William Howell Reed used his brandy flask to restore the wounded sufficiently to secure their names and last messages. When no last words were obtainable, those at home were often distraught." Nurse Jane Stuart Woolsey says, in *Hospital Days,* she regularly received messages for more information. She quotes one "J. R." as writing: "If I could know what his thoughts were as he went away from earth." "B. M." wrote to her saying, "[L]et me know if he was conscious of his situation, his last words and feelings, and all his sayings in his last hours." Perhaps in a time when bodies were buried hastily far from home, the last words were a means of the family realizing and accepting the loved one's death. So strong and wide-spread was the desire for last words that the topic became the subject of contemporary poems such as "Is That Mother" and songs such as "The Dying Confederate's Last Words" in which the dying soldier says:

"Tell them I tried to walk the ways of peace and truth;
O! tell my mother kind the words that she has given,
Have led her wayward child to Jesus and to heaven."

What does today's reader want from these last words? Civil War soldier Benjamin Abbott, confronted with dead and dying soldiers after a battle, wrote, "[I]n the hour of victory we soldiers were touched with pity for these wounded and dying enemies. It was not the place to discuss right and wrong: it was simply a question of humanity." (*Dear Mother: Don't grieve about me. If I get killed, I'll only be dead,* Beehive Press.) In part, we listen to Last Words with a desire to know the person, in the same way that Nurse Margaret Breckinridge, confronted with the wounded Vicksburg soldiers, looked into the eyes of her companion: "I took one long look into Mrs. C.'s eyes, to see how much strength and courage was hidden in them." How much strength and courage is hidden in a person's last words?

We are, from a distance, like those soldiers lined up to witness an execution. As the condemned pass by, "their countenances are closely scanned by every soldier, eager to read therefrom the emotions of the soul within." (Alotta, *Civil War Justice*.)

Recently, a radio host requested listeners to phone in with their responses to the question: "What would you want your last words to be?" Why do we care? Does death bestow significance on last words that ordinary words lack? Do we, in the face of death, become more articulate, more profound? Do the last words sum up a lifetime of contemplation and philosophizing? We like to think so. In the final analysis, Last Words are a mirror in which we may glimpse our own humanity, the strength of our courage. Shakespeare, when he wrote *Hamlet,* understood that the test of a person's philosophy is the fact of death. After that, as Hamlet says, "The rest is silence."

G. W. R.
February, 2001

Author's Note: No attempt has been made to re-tell the stories of the battles in which these individuals fell. Nor has there been any attempt to discuss strategy or maneuvers. Each entry begins with the individual's name followed by his rank, army, place and date of death. In a few instances I have taken the liberty of placing in quotation marks words which are not recorded in quotation marks in the historical sources, but which were, to my mind, accurate records of the individual's last words. These are clearly marked with * and the reader may check the sources which are listed in the bibliography to determine whether my presumptions are justified. Each individual is listed in the index and cross-referenced with the bibliography.

"And in this harsh world draw thy breath in pain,
To tell my story."
--Hamlet
William Shakespeare

PRELUDE TO WAR

In the years preceding the actual conflict, many individuals became entangled in the commercial and idealistic conflicts between the north and south. The struggle to either preserve or destroy the institution of slavery became focused on the territories that were on the verge of statehood. At times, most notably in Kansas and Missouri, the arguments exploded into violence.

National Archives

To his dying breath, John C. Calhoun fought for Southern rights.

JOHN CALDWELL CALHOUN

Senator

Washington, D. C., March 31, 1850

Staunch defender of the Southern cause against Northern commercialism, Calhoun attended Senate sessions voicing his anti-Northern sentiments though his health was so bad that in the last few months of his life he fainted several times in the Senate chambers. Near the end he expressed a concern that many Southerners shared:

> "The South! The poor South! God knows what will become of her!"

THOMAS W. BARBER

Civilian

Near Lawrence, Kansas, December 6, 1855

A free-state advocate, Barber joined other free-staters in Lawrence to resist pro-slavery forces that were attempting to assert authority over this basically free-state community. As tensions appeared to be lessening, Barber and his brother, with the intention of visiting Barber's wife, left Lawrence. Three miles out, they encountered pro-slavery horsemen who ordered them to return. When the brothers refused, Barber was shot in the side and the horsemen quickly rode away. With a "faint, sickly smile" he said,

"That fellow hit me."

He rode a little further, slipped from his horse and died on the road.

ONE OF ELEVEN

Civilian

Trading Post, Kansas, May 19, 1858

When Captain Charles A. Hamilton invaded the hamlet of Trading Post to rid the territory of his anti-slavery enemies, he had only partial success, capturing a group of civilians. From his prisoners, eleven were selected by Hamilton to be executed in a nearby gulch. When the prisoners were lined up, one of the eleven unflinchingly said,

"Gentlemen, if you are going to shoot, take good aim."

Some of the reluctant executioners did not take the advice for, although ten men were hit, only five of the eleven were killed in the volley.

National Archives

Abolitionist John Brown spoke his last words from the gallows.

JOHN BROWN

Abolitionist

Charles Town, (West) Virginia, December 2, 1859

After attacking and capturing the arsenal at Harper's Ferry on October 16, 1859, Brown, the most famous and aggressive abolitionist of his time, was captured, tried and convicted of murder, conspiracy and treason against the State of Virginia.

He was sentenced to death on the gallows. On the day of the execution he gave a note to one of his guards:

> "I John Brown am now quite certain that the crimes of this guilty land will never be purged away but with blood."

A military guard, which included the future presidential assassin John Wilkes Booth, prevented spectators from coming too close to the gallows. Brown reacted:

> "I am sorry citizens have been kept out."

With the noose around his neck and a white hood on his head, Brown was asked by the jailer to step onto the trap. Brown told him,

> "You must lead me—I cannot see."

After a five-minute delay, the jailer asked the patient Brown if he were tired. His last words before the trap was sprung were:

> "No, not tired—but don't keep me waiting longer than necessary."

SUMNER HENRY NEEDHAM

Corporal USA

Baltimore, Maryland, April 28, 1861

As Union troops passed through the city of Baltimore on April 19th, angry citizens stopped the train and attacked the troops with bottles and bricks. Needham of the 6th Massachusetts suffered a severe injury in the Baltimore Riot and died in hospital nine days later. On the morning of the attack, Needham said to a fellow soldier,

> "We shall have trouble today and I shall not get out of it alive. Promise me if I fall that my body shall be sent home."

ST. LOUIS PROTESTOR

St. Louis, Missouri, May 10, 1861

Unwilling to allow the state arsenal to fall into southern hands, Captain Nathaniel Lyon with the U. S. Reserve Corps, known as the German St. Louis Home Guard, secured the arsenal and then captured Camp Jackson on the outskirts of St. Louis. The prisoners, Missouri State Militia, were marched down Grand Avenue to the dismay of the outraged Missouri citizens, many of them southern sympathizers. Protestors began taunting the German troops, shouting,

> "Damn the Dutch!"

Violence erupted, thirty citizens being killed.

STEPHEN ARNOLD DOUGLAS

Senator

Chicago, Illinois, June 3, 1861

A Democratic politician from Illinois known as "The Little Giant", Douglas believed that the slavery issue could be solved by compromise, each state determining its own status. Unsupported by the South, he lost his bid for the United States Presidency to Lincoln. Dying of typhoid at the age of forty-eight, on his deathbed he directed a comment to his sons:

> "Tell them to obey the laws and support the Constitution of the United States."

National Archives

Even on his deathbed Stephen Douglas supported the Union.

FIRST MAN SHOT

Harper's Weekly

ELMER EPHRAIM ELLSWORTH
Colonel, USA
Alexandria, Virginia, May 24, 1861

The day before he gained national fame for being the first man shot in the civil war, Ellsworth wrote a letter to his parents. After his much publicized and much lamented death, the letter was printed on memorial envelopes and widely distributed.

"Washington May 1861

My Dear Father and Mother—The regiment is ordered to move across the river to night. We have no means of knowing what reception we are to meet with. I am inclined to the opinion that our entrance to the city of Alexandria will be hotly contested, as I am informed a large force have arrived there to day. Should this happen, my dear parents, it may be my lot to be injured in some manner. Whatever may happen, cherish the consolation that I was engaged in the performance of a sacred duty; and tonight, thinking over the probabilities of tomorrow and the occurrences of the past, I am perfectly content to accept whatever my fortune may be, confident that He who noteth even the fall of a sparrow, will have some purpose even in the fate of one like me. My darling and ever loved parents, good by. God bless, protect and care for you.

Elmer."

After leading the Fire Zouaves—Eleventh New York—into Alexandria as part of the defense of Washington, Ellsworth and his men marched toward the telegraph office. However, seeing a Confederate flag atop the Marshall House, he said,

"Boys, we must have that flag!"

Making his way to the top of the Marshall House he captured the flag which proprietor Jackson had sworn would never be removed. On his way down the stairs Ellsworth, displaying the flag, met Jackson and said,

"I have a trophy!"

Jackson immediately shot Ellsworth in the heart with his double barrel shotgun and was, in turn, killed by a Federal soldier.

Library of Congress

The Marshall House in Alexandria, Virginia where Ellsworth was killed.

BATTLE OF BIG BETHEL

THEODORE WINTHROP
Major USA
Big Bethel, Virginia, June 10, 1861

Searching for a weak spot in the Confederate defenses, Winthrop led his men forward; then, standing atop a fence, he waved his sword and encouraged an assault. Just before a bullet toppled him from the fence, he shouted,

> "Rally, boys, rally! Come on, boys! One charge and the day is ours!"

Harper's Weekly

John T. Greble: "Let me die as a brave and honorable man."

JOHN T. GREBLE
Lieutenant USA
Big Bethel, Virginia, June 10, 1861

The day before he was killed, Greble wrote two notes, one to a friend and one to his wife.

To his friend:

> "Camp Butler, Newport News, Virginia, June 9.
>
> It is a delightful Sabbath morning—it has a Sabbath feeling about it. If you had lost the run of the week, such a day as to-day would tell you it was the sabbath. The camp is unusually quiet, and its stillness broken by little except the organ tones of some of the Massachusetts men, who are on the beach, singing devotional airs.
>
> I hope that I may be given courage and good judgement enough to do well my duty in any

> circumstances in which I may be placed. As far as I can see, there is not much danger to be incurred in this campaign. At present, both sides seem better inclined to talking than fighting. If talking could settle it, by giving the supremacy forever to the general government, I think it would be better than civil war; but that talking can settle it, I do not believe."

To his wife:

> "May God bless you, my darling, and grant you a happy and peaceful life. May the good father protect you and me, and grant that we may live happily together. God give me strength, wisdom and courage. If I die, let me die as a brave and honorable man: let no stain of dishonor hang over me or you."

Greble and his men coolly fired their artillery piece even though they were in the most exposed position. After being hit by an exploding shell, the second last shot fired by the enemy, he said,

"Sergeant! Take command—go ahead."

BATTLE OF FIRST BULL RUN

SULLIVAN BALLOU
Major, USA
Manassas, Virginia, July 21, 1861
Sensing his fate, Ballou wrote a last letter to his wife.

"Camp Clark, Washington
July 14th, 1861

My very dear Sarah,

The indications are very strong that we shall move in a few days-- perhaps tomorrow.

Lest I shall not be able to write to you again, I feel impelled to write a few lines that may fall under your eye when I shall be no more.

Our movement may be one of a few days duration and full of pleasure, and it may be one of severe conflict and death to me. "Not my will, but Thine O God be done." If it is necessary that I should fall on the battlefield for my Country, I am ready. I have no misgivings about, or lack of confidence in, the cause in which I am engaged and my courage does not halt or falter.

I know how strongly American Civilization now leans on the triumph of the Government, and how great a debt we owe to those who went before us through the blood and suffering of the Revolution, and I am willing, perfectly willing, to lay down all my joys in this life to help maintain this Government and to pay that debt. But my dear wife, when I know that with my own joys I lay down nearly all of yours and replace them in this life with cares and sorrows, when after having eaten for long years the bitter fruit of orphanage myself I must offer it as the only sustenance to my dear little children, is it weak or dishonorable that while the banner of my purpose floats calmly and proudly in the breeze, underneath my unbounded love for you my darling wife and children, shall struggle in fierce though useless contest with my love of Country?

I cannot describe to you my feelings on this calm summer Sabbath night when two thousand men are sleeping around me, many of them enjoying the last, perhaps, before that of death, and I am suspicious that death is creeping behind me with his fatal dart while I am communing with God, My Country and Thee. I have sought most closely and diligently and often in my breast for a wrong motive in thus hazarding the happiness of all those I loved and I could find none. A pure love of my Country and the principles I have often advocated before the people, another name of honor that I love more than I fear death, has called upon me and I have obeyed.

Sarah, my love for you is deathless. It seems to bind me in mighty cables that nothing but Omnipotence could break and my love of country comes over me like a strong wind and bears me irresistibly on with all these chains to the battlefield.

The memories of all the blissful moments I have spent with you come creeping over me and I feel most deeply grateful to God and you that I have enjoyed them so long and how hard it is for me to give them up and burn to ashes the hopes of future years when God Willing we might still have lived and loved together and seen our sons grow up to honorable manhood around us.

I know I have but few and small claims upon Divine Providence but something whispers to me, perhaps it is the wafted prayer of my little Edgar that I shall return to my loved ones unharmed. If I do not my dear Sarah never forget how much I love you and when my last breath escapes me on the battlefield I shall whisper your name. Forgive my many faults and the many pains I have caused you. How thoughtless, how foolish I have often times been. How gladly would I wash out with my tears every little spot upon your happiness and struggle with all the misfortunes of this world to shield you and my dear children from harm but I cannot. I must watch you from the spirit land and hover near you while you buffet the storms with your precious little freight and wait with sad patience till we meet to part no more. But Oh Sarah if the dead can come back to this earth and flit unseen around those they love, I shall always be near you in the gladdest day and in the darkest night amidst your happiest scenes and gloomiest hours, always, always and if there be a soft breeze upon your cheeks it shall be my breath, or the cool air cools your throbbing temple, it shall be my spirit passing by.

Sarah, do not mourn me dead, think I am gone and wait for me, for we shall meet again.

As for my little boys, they will grow up as I have grown and never know a father's love and care, little Willie is too young to remember me long and my blue-eyed Edgar will keep my frolics with him among the dimmest memories of his childhood.

Sarah, I have unbounded confidence in your maternal care and your development of their character and feel that God will bless you in your holy work.

Tell my two mothers I call God's blessing upon them.

Oh Sarah I want for you there come to me and lead thither my children.

Sullivan"

He was killed at First Bull Run one week later, his leg shattered by a cannon ball that killed his horse.

IRISH COLOR BEARER

Manassas, Virginia, July 21, 1861

As the 69th New York State Militia, partially composed of Irish-Americans, waited for an opportunity to attack a Confederate battery that was keeping them pinned down, the regiment's colonel ordered the lowering of the regimental green banner that was being used as a target by Confederate sharpshooters. The Color Bearer responded to the order by saying,

"Don't ask me that, colonel. I'll never lower it!"

The next moment, a sharpshooter's bullet pierced his heart. The next color bearer was also killed before the banner was lowered.

JAMES CAMERON

Colonel USA

Manassas, Virginia, July 21, 1861

Brother to the Secretary of War, Colonel Cameron led the 79th New York in an optimistic charge that gave the soldiers a temporary sense of victory. He shouted,

"Come on, boys! The rebels are in full retreat!"

Moments later, Cameron was killed by a ball in the heart.

FRANCIS S. BARTOW

Colonel CSA

Manassas, Virginia, July 21, 1861

Leading the men of the 7th Georgia in a counter-attack, Bartow was shot in the chest. As the battle raged, he encouraged his men with his dying words, referring to the regimental banner:

"They have killed me, but boys, never give it up!"

DEFIANT CONFEDERATE OFFICER

Manassas, Virginia, July 21, 1861

Standing on an embankment near a cannon as Federal soldiers advanced, the officer, waving his sword over his head, yelled out a challenge,

"Come on, sons of bitches!"

Alonzo Allen Kingsbury of the 1st Massachusetts took careful aim and put a bullet through the Confederate Officer's heart.

FREDERICK DAVIDSON

Corporal CSA

Manassas Junction, July 21, 1861

Davidson of Company H, the 4th Virginia Infantry, and other members of the Rockbridge Rifles, lay on the battlefield for three and a half hours before being ordered to advance. In the charge, which drove back the Federals, Davidson was mortally wounded. Dying, he requested that his body be buried on the battlefield. He sent his last message to his mother, saying,

"Tell my mother I died for a glorious cause."

Though buried on the field, his remains were later removed to Stonewall Jackson cemetery.

WILLIE L.

Private USA

Centreville, Virginia, July 21, 1861

Wounded in the breast, Willie L. was taken from the Bull Run battlefield to the field hospital in the Stone Church in Centreville. Near death, he indicated a package and said to a nurse,

> "I wish you to take that. Keep it until you get to Washington, and then, if it is not too much trouble, I want you to write to mother and tell her how I was wounded, and that I died trusting in Jesus."

With his fingers he made a sign to cut a lock of his hair. He died as the chaplain was praying.

SINGING SOLDIER

USA

Centreville, Virginia, July 21, 1861

In the field hospital at the Stone Church in Centreville, this soldier asked Nurse Emma E. Edmonds,

"Do you think I'll die before morning?"

When she asked him if he were afraid to die, he responded,

"Oh, no. I shall soon be asleep in Jesus."

He died as he quietly sang,

"Asleep in Jesus, blessed sleep."

National Archives

The Stone Church in Centreville near the Bull Run battlefield was used as a field hospital.

JUNE 1861~FEBRUARY 1862

WILLIAM P. SWAIN

Private USA

Near Baltimore, Maryland, June 29, 1861

Substituting for an absent gunner during a drill, twenty-four year old Swain was bending over to seize the trail handspike when the hammer of the revolver in his breast pocket struck the handspike. After the revolver fired, he exclaimed,

"I am shot!"

He hastily tore open his shirt, then said,

"No, I am not!"

He collapsed immediately, the bullet having passed through his chest.

CHARLES D. DREUX

Lieutenant Colonel CSA

Newport News, Virginia, July 5, 1861

At midnight, Dreux led his men to a spot from which they could ambush a Federal foraging party. Near dawn, hidden in the brush by the road, the men could hear the approach of the enemy. Dreux warned his men,

"They are coming!"

Concerned that his men might fire too soon and ruin the ambush, Dreux said,

"Boys, steady."

After some minutes, when the enemy did not appear, Dreux sent out scouts and waited. As Dreux and several others stood by the road, they were surprised to see several enemy soldiers appear. In the shooting that immediately followed, Dreux and one private were killed. The enemy retreated without falling into the ambush.

ROBERT SELDEN GARNETT

Brigadier General CSA

Carrick's Ford, Virginia, July 13, 1861

In his first engagement, Garnett stopped with ten raw recruits to delay the enemy. He told an officer,

"This is a good place behind this driftwood to post skirmishers."

After posting his men, observing that they were nervous under fire, he stepped out in view of the enemy, saying,

"The men need a little example."

He walked slowly as sharpshooters fired at him. Just as he gave the order to withdraw, he was killed.

INEBRIATED JOKER

Private, USA

Washington, D. C., July 3, 1861

Returning to camp after the time specified, the slightly inebriated New York soldier, when challenged by the guard to identify himself, responded jokingly,

"A secessionist."

The inexperienced guard shot the man in the head.

CORPORAL

Sigel's Home Guards, USA

Wilson's Creek, Missouri, August 10, 1861

Watching the approach of soldiers dressed in gray, the Corporal and General Sigel thought the men were Federals, the 1st Iowa Infantry who also wore gray. Sent to confirm the identity of the men, the Corporal approached the group's leader who asked the Corporal to identify his outfit. As soon as he uttered his response,

"Sigel's regiment,"

the Corporal realized he was talking to a Confederate officer. Though he tried to shoot, the Corporal was immediately fired upon and killed.

Harper's Weekly

Outnumbered, Nathaniel Lyon was killed attempting one more attack at Wilson's Creek.

NATHANIEL LYON

Brigadier General USA

Wilson's Creek, Missouri, August 10, 1861

Though believing his smaller force was beaten in the battle to determine if Missouri would be a base for Union forces, Lyon, wounded in the leg and head, was convinced to attempt one more attack. Trying to plug a hole in the line, he borrowed a horse and encouraged his men:

"Come on, my brave boys! I will lead you! Forward!"

He was immediately hit in the side. Dismounting, he collapsed in his orderly's arms, saying,

"Lehman, I am killed."

COMPANY G SOLDIER

USA

September, 1861

Going through the arms manual with a careless companion who thought the rifle he was using was not loaded, the Company G soldier gave the order

"Ready! Aim! Fire!"

and his companion shot him in the chest.

JAMES(?) ABBOTT

Private USA

Near Cheat Mountain, [West] Virginia, October 3, 1861

Carrying a furlough pass, three twists of braided hair from his sisters and a letter to his sisters, Abbott from Indiana left camp on Cheat Mountain to attack the Confederate forces camped ten miles away on Greenbrier River. In the letter, now lost but paraphrased in the diary of Confederate James E. Hall, Abbot wrote to his sisters:

> "[I will] not start home as soon as [I] expected, as the army [is] going down the mountain to whip the rebels, and [I am] going to accompany it so [I can] tell [you] about it when [I come] home." *

During the attack Abbott was hit by a cannon ball. After the battle, his body with the letter was found by Confederate soldiers.

LIEUTENANT 6TH OHIO

Elkwater, West Virginia, October 5, 1861

Camped with his fellows on one side of a stream, the Lieutenant observed on the other side of the stream the return to camp of unruly and undisciplined Indiana soldiers, one of whom raised his rifle to shoot at a snake in the stream.

Realizing the danger to his own men, the Lieutenant stepped forward to forestall the shot.

"For God's sake, don't fire!"

Ignoring the officer, the Indiana soldier fired, the ball ricocheting off the water and striking the Lieutenant in the chest.

EDWARD DICKINSON BAKER

Colonel USA

Ball's Bluff, Virginia, October 21, 1861

At one point in the battle Baker, former Oregon senator and friend of Lincoln, dismounted and walked along the line of the 20th Massachusetts ordering the men to lie down. When a soldier pointed out the fact that Baker was not lying down, Baker responded,

"No, my son, and when you get to be a United States senator, you will not lie down either."

Later in the day, striding in front of his hard pressed men, Baker ordered reinforcements; then, seeing across the field a Confederate horseman apparently hit, Baker said,

"See, he falls."

At that moment, a Confederate private shot Baker four times with a cavalry revolver.

Harper's Weekly

The death of Edward D. Baker at Ball's Bluff saddened Baker's friend Abraham Lincoln and shocked Washington.

WILLIE GROUT

Lieutenant USA

Ball's Bluff, Virginia, October 21, 1861

As the Federal army retreated across the Potomac River, Grout took a boatload of soldiers to the Maryland shore. Returning, he was told to make his way back. Finding no boats remaining, he began to swim across. Approximately seventy-five yards from the Maryland shore he was hit in the head by a musket ball. Swimming closer to the shore, he said,

"Tell Company D I should have made it!"

Then he disappeared in the river.

FRIEND WITH THE COUNTERSIGN

CSA

Western Virginia, November(?), 1861

When the advance guard of the Second Virginia, moving at night, encountered a picket, they were challenged to identify themselves. Believing they had met a friendly scouting party, the spokesman responded to the challenge with,

"Friends, with the countersign."

Asked to give the countersign, he hesitated, then said,

"Mississippi."

Asked to whom he belonged, he replied,

"To the Second Virginia regiment."

When his destination was demanded, he responded,

"Along the ridge."

Having been cooperative, he decided to obtain some information himself. He asked the figure in the moonlight,

"Where are you going?"

The answer, in the form of a bullet, was final.

FELIX KIRK ZOLLICOFFER

General CSA

Mill Springs, Kentucky, January 19, 1862

In the confusion of the fighting, General Zollicoffer, wearing a light drab overcoat buttoned to the chin, rode past his lines into enemy territory. Riding slowly by an enemy regiment, he was approached by Federal Colonel S. S. Fry who mistakenly thought Zollicoffer was a Federal officer. Perhaps confused, perhaps in hopes of deceiving Fry until he could make his escape, Zollicoffer calmly said to Fry,

"We must not shoot our own men."

After Fry agreed, Zollicoffer pointed in the direction of the Confederate lines and said,

"Those are our men."

Zollicoffer watched as Fry, unable to see any men in that direction, turned off the road. Moments later, when another Confederate officer suddenly appeared and shot at Fry, Zollicoffer spurred his horse to return to his lines. However, Fry and several men of the Fourth Kentucky fired at Zollicoffer, three shots hitting him, one from a musket striking him in the heart. Fry, whose pistol shot also hit him, is often credited with killing Zollicoffer.

Harper's Weekly

Perhaps because of poor eyesight, Felix Zollicoffer was caught behind enemy lines.

DESPERATE MOMENT AT VALVERDE

SAMUEL A. LOCKRIDGE

Major CSA

Near Fort Craig, New Mexico, February 21, 1862

In the Battle of Valverde, Colonel Canby's twenty-five hundred soldiers fought for the Union against General Sibley's three thousand Texans. Just as the Union forces seemed to prevail, Confederate Colonel Thomas Green led a desperate charge toward McRae's battery. Major Lockridge, at the forefront of the charge, reached the battery, put his hand victoriously on the cannon and said,

"This is mine!"

Shot immediately, he slumped, saying,

"Go on, my boys; don't stop here."

ALEXANDER McRAE

Captain USA

Near Fort Craig, New Mexico, February 21, 1862

As Major Lockridge's boys swarmed toward McRae's artillery piece, McRae stood his ground. Seeing Lockridge reach out and touch the cannon, McRae shouted,

"Shoot the son of a bitch!"

Though his order was followed, McRae died in the futile defense of his artillery.

BATTERY BOY

USA

Near Fort Craig, New Mexico, February 21, 1862

Outnumbered and faced with a retreat to Fort Craig, Canby's gunners, knowing that the battery would have to be abandoned, refused to leave until the Confederates overwhelmed them. One of the young men manning the battery leaped onto the ammunitions supply, shouted,

"Victory or death!"

and fired his pistol into the magazine causing an explosion that killed the Battery Boy and several attackers.

BATTLE OF SHILOH

EDWARD SAXE

Captain USA

Shiloh, Tennessee, April 6, 1862

Meeting Colonel David Moore and five companies of the 21st Missouri at approximately 7 a.m., Saxe threw off his coat and said to his men,

"Boys, we will fall in on the right and lead them."

As he led his men across an old cotton field toward the enemy, Saxe and his sergeant were cut down by the first volley.

"CURSING CONFEDERATE"

Private CSA

Shiloh, Tennessee, April 6, 1862

Under heavy fire, several members of Shaver's brigade took cover behind a fallen tree that offered only limited protection. Seeing two of his comrades killed even as they huddled behind the tree, he said,

"It is getting too warm, boys!"

After throwing out a few curses at officers for keeping the men in such a dangerous position, he rose up and was immediately killed by a ball in the forehead.

EVERETT PEABODY

Colonel USA

Shiloh, Tennessee, April 6, 1862

As his camp was over-run by attacking Confederates, his men fighting as individuals rather than an organized unit, the thirty-one year old Peabody rode his horse between the tents and shouted,

"Stand to it yet!"

Wounded in the head, thigh, neck and body, he was finally killed by a ball that struck him in the face.

FEDERAL YOUTH

Shiloh, Tennessee, April 6, 1862

After the fighting, the mortally wounded boy lay in an officer's tent beside a Confederate corpse. As he approached death, he whispered to an officer who was holding his hand,

"Tell mother where you found me—on the front line."

ALBERT SYDNEY JOHNSTON

General, CSA

Shiloh, Tennessee, April 6, 1862

After a successful charge that drove back the Union forces, he returned smiling, his uniform torn by bullets and his boot sole ripped in half. He boasted,

"They didn't trip me up this time!"

Suddenly he lost strength, nearly falling from his horse. When an aide inquired if he were hurt, he replied,

"Yes, and I fear seriously."

Unaware that his life-blood was flowing from a severed artery in his knee, he ordered his physician, who would have known to apply a tourniquet, to attend to the prisoners of war. He died shortly after saying,

"These men were our enemies a moment ago. They are our prisoners now. Take care of them."

Harper's Weekly

Albert Sydney Johnston bled to death from what appeared to be a minor wound.

MISSOURI YOUTH

Private USA

Shiloh, Tennessee, April 6, 1862

As the Union soldiers retreated from their camp, this soldier of the 18th Missouri was shot in the abdomen, the wound allowing eighteen inches of his intestine to protrude. As the stomach muscles contracted, the intestines were squeezed. He cried out in pain to the chaplain who tried to replace the intestines,

"I feel as if my bowels are in boiling water!"

Under the pressure of the attacking Confederates the chaplain was forced to leave the young man to die in the hands of the enemy.

PARKER BAGLEY

Sergeant USA

Shiloh, Tennessee, April 6, 1862

Aiding wounded Lieutenant Crooker across a ravine during the mid-afternoon retreat, Bagley, already wounded in the left arm, used his right arm to support Crooker. When Crooker finally noticed Bagley's wounded arm, Bagley said,

> "That doesn't amount to anything. Lean on me as heavily as you have a mind to--"

Just then a musket ball seared Crooker's back and killed Bagley.

CONFUSED COLONEL

USA

Shiloh, Tennessee, April 6, 1862

As the Federals retreated in disorder, a Union officer, possibly a Colonel, rode up in confusion to a Confederate regiment and shouted,

> "Boys, for God's sake, stop firing! You are killing your friends!"

Seeing his error, he tried to ride away but was easily killed by his "friends."

BEN WEBER

Corporal ?, CSA

Shiloh, Tennessee, April 7, 1862

With the Captain and First Lieutenant both wounded, Weber led the men into devastating fire. Shot in the chest, he fell, saying,

> "Uncle Nat good bye. Give them all my love at home."

"ANOTHER POOR FELLOW"

USA

Shiloh, Tennessee, April 7, 1862

Wounded in the fierce fighting of the day before, he and other dying soldiers crawled to a ravine for shelter. As the battle continued, these men were bypassed by fighting soldiers who had no time to attend to the pleas of one who begged to be put out of his misery and another who kept repeating,

> "O God, have mercy! O God! O God!"

SHILOH SOLDIER

Private, USA

Aboard the City of Memphis, Mississippi River, April, 1862

Wounded at Shiloh, the young soldier had his leg amputated. Comforting him in his weak state, a nurse sang "Nearer My God, to Thee". Just before dropping off into his final sleep, he responded,

> "Oh, I have heard that sung hundreds of times, but never before did it sound to me so beautiful."

CHESTER A. BUCKLAND

Private USA

Cincinnati, Ohio, April 18, 1862

After escaping from Confederate pickets, twenty-year old Buckland from Ohio expressed his elation in a letter to his mother. The next day, April 6th, he was mortally wounded in the battle of Shiloh and died twelve days later on the steamboat as he was being transported from Cairo to Cincinnati.

> "Camp Shiloh, West Tennessee
> Saturday, April 5, 1862
> Dearest Mother:
>
> You may glory in us now. Yesterday, while drilling about a mile from here, our pickets were fired upon. In a very few moments the Seventy-second was on its way to battle in a double quick step, company B in the rear. When we arrived at a convenient place, we were deployed as skirmishers, and were to try and surround the rebels. We wandered along a couple of miles. I and Henry were near the end of the company. The company was in groups of four, each group twenty paces apart. An order was given to rally on first group, when the front commenced to fire, but ceased before we could get up. We wandered in a body for near an hour, making frequent halts. Every ear was listening and every eye watching for sound or sight of the enemy. Nearly an hour from the first fire we got sight of them again, and nearly all got a chance to fire. We think one was killed or badly wounded. Here we found there were more than we thought, and so we retreated to a kind of pen built of rails, and then to a big tree on the brow of a ravine. In a little time the rebel cavalry rode up in sight, and then the fight began. I could hear the balls go "whip" through the air, and hear them strike the trees around us. There were a hundred and fifty rebels

against forty-four of us! Once in a while one would drop from his horse or a horse would fall dead or wounded.

We would load, run up where we could see, drop on our knees, take aim and fire, and then run back to load. In this manner we made them believe there were a good many more than there were of us.

In this part of the fight two of our men were wounded, Charles H. Bennet, in the right leg and James Titsword through the left breast above the heart. When we had fought about three-fourths of an hour, it commenced to rain and hail, which made it difficult to load without wetting the powder. Then the rebels retreated. In a very little time it rained so hard we could not see more than a couple of rods, which was just exactly the time for them to ride onto us and cut us to pieces. We threw out guards to watch for them. I never knew it to rain so hard. When the rain had ceased, we saw them forming on a sort of prairie beyond the reach of our Enfields. In a short time they gave a great shout and advanced on us. As soon as they were within good reach, we commenced to drop on them again. They had been reinforced to about four or five hundred, beside what may have been in reserve. We fought here about a quarter of an hour more, during which three more were wounded and several had holes shot in their clothes, one having a thumb broke, two shots through his arm, one through his clothes and one in his boot. Now was the desperate time. The rebels fired a volley, drew sabres, and began to advance. They were on three sides of us. Our hearts began to sink. We rallied around the old white oak, each one grasping his gun with its powder-stained bayonet, and determined to give as good as he got. How fierce we felt. Our last chance seemed gone, when a volley sounded in the rear of the rebels. It was the Seventy-second! How loud the hurrahs sounded then! It was the sweetest music I ever heard! The rebels turned and fled. We were saved. We fired as long as we could reach them and then took Titsword in care, and then we went over to where part of the rebels had been. We found two mortally wounded ones. Our Enfields make wicked holes. The first was a young boy about eighteen. He was afraid of us and wanted to know what we would do with him. We promised to take care of him, as we would one of our own men. He was assured of this, for one wanted to kill him, but we raked him so the boy was encouraged. The other was a man about twenty-five. We carried them as far as the pickets, where we had to leave them, for we could carry them no farther. Each one said there were about four of five hundred of them. They were from Alabama, were well dressed and pretty well armed. These two men died last night. The rebels had carried all their wounded and dead away, but our cavalry say they saw about twenty dead rebels in the woods, and there must have been many wounded. I saw four dead horse.

Company A passed over the ground where our heaviest fire was aimed, and found a great many sabres, pistols, guns, blankets and everything they couldn't take away. They had a battery not far from where we were, and the cavalry followed them nearly into it. I have heard our men took two pieces of artillery, but am not certain if it be true. None on our side were killed, but Major Crockett, I fear, is a prisoner. The last seen of him, he was riding like a flash through the woods, followed by a dozen rebel horsemen. He had no arms with him, and couldn't fight them. A sergeant and a corporal were taken prisoner from Company H. Company H had four wounded, one the color-sergeant, old Dr. Gessner's son. He was taken prisoner and told to climb behind one of the rebels, which he would not do. The rebel drew a revolver and snapped it at him, but it missed fire. He ran while the rebel was cocking it again, when the fellow shot and hit him in the shoulder. Our men took nine or ten prisoners, who said they hadn't thought we could shoot so well. We must have killed about as many as there were of us, for every man took aim, and there are some who don't miss often. Orin England and Eugene Rawson were with our company, and neither one of them had even a pistol; but as soon as Titswood was wounded, Orin took his gun and cartridge box and fought well, while Eugene stood up with the boys and talked and laughed, and told them to keep cool and take good aim. It was no light matter to stand up unarmed, and a lot of fellows shooting at one. While we were bringing in the wounded there was a heavy battle not far from where we fought. Our fight will probably not appear in the papers, but we had a hard struggle against most fearful odds. Ten to one is a great disadvantage. Two minutes more, and company B, Seventy-second Ohio Volunteer Infantry, would have been no more. We would have all been killed, for each one would have died fighting. It would have been a barren victory, for there would have been a dead rebel or two for every one of us. Our bayonets were fixed, and they are sorry things to run upon. We were willing to stop fighting. How soon we will have another fight I don't know, but any minute the long roll may sound for the battle. We may fight and die; but, mother, your sons will never quail.

It is getting too dark to write, so I must close. Good-bye, dear mother, and remember if I die it is for my country.

Your son,
Chester A. Buckland"

WILLIAM POPE

Private CSA

Corinth, Mississippi, April ?, 1862

Wounded at Shiloh, Pope suffered through an arm amputation. After the surgery he was quite cheerful, commenting,

> "Poor Elston boasted that he was sure to come through the war with nothing worse than a slight wound and here it is that he is gone and I am left with the honorable wound."

However, gangrene set in, requiring further amputation. He died shortly after. On the day of his death he said to Johnny Green,

> "Johnnie, if a boy dies for his country, the glory is his forever, isn't it?"

MAY 1862~JUNE 1862

GEORGE T. WARD

Colonel, CSA

Near Williamsburg, Virginia, May 5, 1862

Coming to relieve another regiment under fire, the 2nd Florida misunderstood, believing that the order to fall back applied to them as well. In the resulting confusion and rout, Colonel Ward tried to rally his fleeing regiment.

> "Floridians, oh, Floridians, is this the way you meet the enemies of your country?"

Struck in the chest by a bullet, the gallant Colonel fell from his horse. He was one of four Floridians killed that day.

RELIGIOUS SOLDIER

USA

Williamsburg, Virginia, May 5(?), 1862

Wounded in the fighting when Yorktown was evacuated, this soldier was comforted by a tired chaplain in a Williamsburg hospital. When he realized the seriousness of his wound he said,

> "I am to die then? And how long?"

Assured by the chaplain that Christ would save him, he responded,

> "Yes, but this is so awfully sudden, awfully sudden!
> And I shall not see my mother."

After a lengthy pause as he came to terms with his dying, he said to the chaplain,

> "I thank you for your courage. The bitterness is over now, and I feel willing to die. Tell my mother—tell her how I longed to see her, but if God will permit me I will be near her. Tell her to comfort all who loved me, to say that I thought of them all. Tell my father that I am glad he gave his consent. Tell my minister, by word or letter, that I thought of him, and that I thank him for all his counsels. Tell him I find that Christ will not desert the passing soul, and that I wish him to give my testimony to the living, that nothing is of real worth but the religion of Jesus. And now, will you pray with me?"

After the chaplain prayed with him, he continued,

"Thank you. I won't trouble you any longer. You are wearied out; go to your rest."

Though exhausted, the chaplain remained with him until he died an hour later.

HIRAM M. OSBORNE

Private USA

Near Corinth, Mississippi, May 11, 1862

While sleeping on the ground, Osborne and other men of Company I, 10th Indiana were awakened before dawn by several horses galloping through camp. The men, including Osborne, sat up and, to frighten the horses away, they shouted,

"Halloooo!"

Going back to sleep, all awoke the next morning except Osborne who had died mysteriously in his sleep.

FEEBLE QUESTIONER

Private USA

Hanover Court House, Virginia, May 27, 1862

When the battle was over, the feeble, wounded private was approached by his colonel who thought the private might want to pass on a dying message to his family. Instead, the dying man asked,

"Colonel, is the day ours?"

Assured it was, he relaxed, said,

"Then I am willing to die"

and waited for death.

GEORGE L. PUTNAM

Private USA

Near Richmond, Virginia, May 31, 1862

Suffering an unexpected attack while in camp, the 10th Massachusetts rushed into battle. While being carried from the field on a stretcher, nineteen-year old Putnam wanted his captain and the world to know that he had measured up to his own standards.

"Tell Captain Parsons I died a soldier."

TWELVE YEAR OLD BOY

CSA

Near Savage Station, Virginia, May 31, 1862

After the day's fighting, the young boy, possibly a drummer boy, lay in the dark camp, pale and barely breathing, his right leg amputated above the knee. A doctor bent over the boy and, taking his pulse, was surprised to discover that the boy was still alive. The boy, opening his eyes, said,

"Yes, sir, I am alive. Will you not send me to my mother?"

Asked for her residence, the boy replied,

"In Sumterville, South Carolina."

Assured that he would be sent home, the dying boy said,

"Well, well, that is kind. I will go to sleep now."

JOSEPH BYNON

CSA

Near Savage Station, Virginia, June 1, 1862

Wounded in the bowels, Bynon, weak from loss of blood, lay on a blanket. Asked by a doctor if he were ready to die, Bynon responded,

"Well, doctor, I should like to live; I love my mother. This will be a great sorrow to her, and I should like to do something for my little nephew and niece. But there is another life, and I know I shall find my mother there. I feel I have been a sinner. In many things I have done very wrong, but ever since the conversion I experienced in Camp Johnson, I have tried to follow my Savior, and now I die trusting. My mind wanders; I find it difficult to think and speak. In praying to God I may not say the things that are right. Doctor, lift up my hands and clasp them together, and pray for me. I will follow you."

He repeated the prayers the doctor spoke; then he added,

"Oh! Lamb of God, who taketh away the sin of the world, take away my sin. Into Thine hand I commend my spirit!"

He thanked the doctor but when the doctor had to become involved in the retreat Bynon begged,

"Doctor, don't leave me."

Placed in an ambulance, he began the journey to Savage Station but died before reaching there.

"H. E. C."

Private USA

Savage Station, Virginia, June 2, 1862

Appearing to be dead on the field after the battle at Savage Station, he opened his eyes to find a fourteen-year old Confederate soldier reaching for his haversack. Asking the boy soldier for water, the dying man added,

"There is a spoon in my haversack."

The oversized spoon engraved "H. E. C." was obviously an important possession. With his enemy's help, he took three drinks from it before he died. The young Confederate carried the spoon with him for the rest of the war.

JAMES MILLER

Colonel USA

Fair Oaks, Virginia, June 1, 1862

Seeing soldiers advancing through the woods, Miller of the 81st Pennsylvania began to give the order,

"Ready, aim..."

but was interrupted by the shout of one of his men who identified the on-coming soldiers as Federals. Miller reacted by ordering,

"Recover arms!"

and then shouted,

"Who are you?"

The response was a chorus of, "Virginians!" and a volley that killed Miller and many of his men.

FRANCIS SWEETSER

Private USA

Fair Oaks, Virginia, June 1, 1862

Wounded in the battle at Fair Oaks, twenty-three year old Sweetser of the 16th Massachusetts, said, shortly before he died as he lay under a large tree at the field hospital,

"Thank God that I am permitted to die for my country. Thank God more yet that I am prepared to die—at least I hope I am."

N. O. HACK

Private, USA

Near Florence, Alabama, June 14, 1862

Suffering from insufficient rations, the soldiers marched through stifling heat and the smothering dust of 30,000 men on the move. Many became sick and a few died. Exhausted, Hack lay down under a tree and gave up. The doctor who reached him too late found a note in the dead man's pocket:

"My name is N. O. Hack, I am from _____ Co., Ohio. If I am killed write to my mother."

NAVAL DEATHS

Though the most famous of the civil war naval engagements occurred between the *Merrimac* and the *Monitor*, there were numerous minor engagements on the coast and the Mississippi River. Gunboats regularly accompanied the transport of men and supplies on the river and occasionally provided long-range support during an assault.

National Archives

"ONE BRAVE FELLOW"

Seaman USN

Near Fort Henry, Tennessee, February 6, 1862

Aboard the gunboat *Essex* during the river attack on Fort Henry, "one brave fellow" (either James Coffey, Dana Wilson or J. P. Breas) was severely scalded when a cannon shot entered the boiler room causing an explosion. The damaged vessel drifted down the Tennessee River away from the battle. An hour or so later, though in pain, he inquired about the outcome of the fight and was told of the victory. Moments before dying, he exclaimed,

"Glory to God!"

NAVAL GUNNER

CSN

Off Newport News, Virginia, March 8, 1862

As the *Patrick Henry* passed Federal shore batteries in an attempt to engage United States Navy ships, she was struck by several shells, one striking the crew of No. 3 gun. His mates wounded, the humble dying Gunner, knowing the action was only beginning, said,

"Never mind me, boys."

JOHN "JACK" ROBINSON

Gun Captain CSN

Off Newport News, Virginia, March 8, 1862

Aboard the Confederate vessel, *Beaufort*, Robinson stood by his gun as the Federal ship, *Congress*, surrendered. Though his mates were leaving the *Beaufort* to escort the wounded prisoners from the *Congress*, Robinson, seeing a nearby Federal gunboat, hesitated, telling his Captain,

"Why, Captain, they can come and take you while we are gone."

Even as the *Beaufort's* men approached the *Congress*, Federal soldiers on shore opened fire, one rifle ball hitting Robinson who had returned to his gun. Taken below, he was later visited by the Captain who asked if there was anything to be done for him. Robinson replied,

"I would like a cup of tea and a pair of clean socks." *

Thus making himself comfortable, he waited for death which came in a few hours.

GEORGE W. COLE

Master's Mate USN

Near Chalmette, Louisiana, April 24, 1862

As the U. S. Steamer *Iroquois* attacked Fort St. Philip and Fort Jackson at the mouth of the Mississippi River, it suffered damage from the guns of the Confederate gunboat, the *McCrae*. Hit by a cannon shot, Cole, Master's Mate aboard the *Iroquois*, died bravely, shouting to the men,

"Don't mind me. Go on with your guns!" *

CHARLES H. SWASEY

Lieutenant USN

Near Donaldsonville, Louisiana, October 4, 1862

About 2 p.m. the U. S. Gunboat *Sciota* was ambushed by well-concealed Confederate artillery. Just after firing his IX-inch gun at the enemy, executive officer Swasey was struck by a shell in the hip. The shell also severed his right hand. Though the ship escaped further damage, young Swasey died about an hour later, saying,

"Tell my mother I tried to be a good man."

HENRY BAKER

Acting Master's Mate, USN

Fort Caswell, North Carolina, February 23, 1863

Aboard the U. S. S. *Monticello,* Baker was killed during an engagement, hit in the right shoulder and also between the eyes by the fifth or sixth shot from the fort. He died leaving behind him a mystery as to his identity. Among his effects were letters, apparently for him but addressed to George Baker and Thomas Furnald. He further complicated the mystery when, with his dying breath, he said,

> "A. C. Barker. Send my things to S. D. Skellton, Charlestown, Massachusetts. I leave all that I have got to my father."

He was buried at sea.

LANCASTER ENGINEER

USN

Near Vicksburg, Mississippi, March 25, 1863

As the gunboats *Lancaster* and *Switzerland* attempted to run the blockade at Vicksburg, the *Lancaster* was hit by a shell. The boiler exploded, severely scalding the engineer and others. Pulled from the water, the engineer immediately tried to attack a crewman who had earlier suggested surrender. The engineer exclaimed,

> "Where's that coward that talked of surrendering? I'll shoot him before I die!"

Visited in the hospital by Mary Livermore later that afternoon, the engineer made his final comments:

> "I did my duty and never talked of surrendering. And I thank God I have no mother, wife, nor child to mourn for me. You may say a prayer for me, a short one, for it's almost over."

ANDREW HULL FOOTE

Rear Admiral USN

New York, New York, June 26, 1863

After successfully aiding General Grant in the capture of Fort Henry, Tennessee, Foote was wounded in the successful taking of Fort Donelson in February, 1862. A year later, the fifty-seven year old Foote died as he was about to take command of the South Atlantic Blockading Squadron. His last words are recorded as:

> "We will have them, North and South....The colored people. Yes, we will have them....We must have charity—charity—charity."

National Archives

Rear Admiral Andrew Hull Foote never recovered from the wound he received at Fort Donelson.

TUNIS CRAVEN

Naval Captain USN

Mobile Bay, Alabama, August 5, 1864

In the attack on Fort Morgan, Craven's ship, the *Tecumseh,* hit a torpedo. As it quickly sank, the pilot and Craven followed several men to the escape hatch ladder. Captain Craven said,

> "After you, Pilot."

The pilot ascended but the Captain and the rest of his men went down with the ship.

SEVEN DAYS' BATTLE

SUFFERING SOLDIER

Private USA

Near Mechanicsville, Virginia, June 25, 1862

In the prelude to the battle at Mechanicsville wounded Federal soldiers were picked up by Confederate soldiers, the Louisiana Tigers, recruited from New Orleans' prisons. One of the wounded Federal privates, in considerable pain, had no sooner said,

"Some one put me out of my misery!"

than a Louisiana Tiger clubbed him to death with his musket butt.

CHRISTIAN SOLDIER

CSA

Near Mechanicsville, Virginia, June 27, 1862

Brought off the battlefield, the mortally wounded soldier repeatedly made the prayer:

"Oh, my Jesus, sweet Jesus, come, take me home!"

WILLIAM SHEARER

Captain CSA

Gaines' Mill, Virginia, June 27, 1862

As the 13th Virginia was ordered forward by General Jackson, Shearer shook hands with a fellow officer and said,

"Goodbye, Captain. I hope to see you soon."

The brigade suffered heavy casualties, Shearer receiving a fatal wound in the head.

CHATHAM ROBERDEAU (BOB) WHEAT

Major CSA

Gaines' Mill, Virginia, June 27, 1862

Wheat was well known as the commanding officer of the notorious Louisiana Tigers. Offered a drink by his friend General Moxley Sorrel just before the charge, Wheat accepted, saying,

"Moxley, something tells old Bob that this is the last drink he'll ever take in this world and he'll take it with you."

In the charge Wheat was shot, and told the men around him,

"Bury me on the field, boys!"

HEZEKIAH EASTON

Captain USA

Gaines' Mill, Virginia, June 27, 1862

Just before the Confederates massed for yet another attack on his battery, Easton dared,

"The enemy shall never take this battery but over my dead body!"

Moments later he died, the Confederates overrunning his guns.

WALTER S. COLBY

Private USA

Gaines' Mill, Virginia, June 27, 1862

Though offered a discharge by a surgeon in Baltimore after he became sick, he insisted on rejoining his regiment saying that he would return home either with the regiment or in a box. Perhaps suffering from tuberculosis, Colby caught up to his regiment and, despite a chronic cough, the thin man kept up on marches and did his duty. At Gaines' Mill, Colby fought bravely until his leg was severely shattered. He rose, standing on his shattered leg, waved his cap and gave three cheers for the Union. Too weak to continue, he fell and said to a fellow soldier who had stopped to aid him,

"I will not live a great while anyhow and I might as well die as I am. You'd better not mind me, but look out for yourself." *

ARMSTEAD

Captain CSA

Gaines's Mill, Virginia, June 27, 1862

As the Confederates charged, Captain Armstead patted his color bearer, Billy, on the shoulder and said,

"Go it, my Billy!"

In the charge, a minie ball struck Billy, passed through his body and killed Captain Armstead as well.

CAREY SMITH

CSA

Savage Station, Virginia, June 29, 1862

Lying in the woods at nightfall with his brother and others of the 21st Mississippi regiment, he put his hand in his jacket and was surprised to find that he was bleeding. Unaware that he had been shot, he had only a moment to look at the blood on his hand and say,

"What does this mean?"

VIRGINIAN REBEL

Private CSA

Frayser's Farm, Virginia, June 30, 1862

As his regiment over-ran an artillery position, this soldier entered into hand to hand combat exclaiming,

> "Surrender, you durned Yanks, to the Sixtieth Virginia!"

A Yankee gunner swung his rammer, smashing the brave Confederate's head.

JOHN CHILDRESS

Private CSA

Frayser's Farm, Virginia, June 30, 1862

In the second last battle of the Seven Days' Battles, John Childress fell on the field and, amid the confusion of the Confederate charge, shouted his last words:

> "I am killed. Tell Ma and Pa goodbye for me."

PEYTON

Major CSA

Malvern Hill, Virginia, July 1, 1862

As the Confederate army fought fiercely to protect Richmond, Peyton led his men into battle, passing his severely wounded fifteen-year old son who cried to him for help. Peyton paused only long enough to say,

> "When we have beaten the enemy, then I will help you. I have here other sons to lead to glory. Forward!"

Major Peyton fell after advancing only a few more paces.

WILLIAM HARRISON ROCKWELL

Private CSA

Malvern Hill, Virginia, July 1, 1862

As the 18th North Carolina regiment charged, twenty-one year old Rockwell, along with his fellows expressed their belief in their cause and their leader by yelling their war cry,

> "Stonewall!"

Rockwell died in the initial charge.

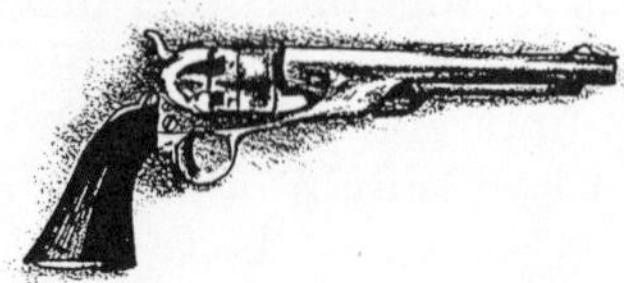

DRISCOLL

Officer CSA

Malvern Hill, Virginia, July 1, 1862

Daring and reckless, Driscoll exposed himself to enemy fire as he urged his men to beat back an enemy advance. Hit by a bullet from a Federal sharpshooter, he fell mortally wounded, and his men, somewhat demoralized, retreated. As the Federals advanced, Driscoll was approached by the sharpshooter who had hit him. As the sharpshooter turned Driscoll onto his back, Driscoll opened his eyes, recognized his killer, and, with his last breath, murmured his name:

"Father."

When the Federal forces renewed the attack, the sharpshooter, Sergeant Driscoll, carelessly charged into the enemy lines and was killed.

TROWBRIDGE

USA

Malvern Hill, Virginia, July 2, 1862

After an exhausting retreat, Trowbridge said to his lieutenant,

"I am so weak and helpless I do not know what I can do further."

Offered a drink of brandy, he refused, saying to the nurse,

"I never take any intoxicating liquor under any circumstances."

Put on guard duty that night, he took the first shift while his relief slept. At midnight, waking the sleepy relief guard who protested that it was too early to switch guards, he whispered,

"Feel the hands of my watch; it is twelve."

An hour and a half later, shaken by his partner, the sleeping Trowbridge merely groaned once and died, apparently from heart failure.

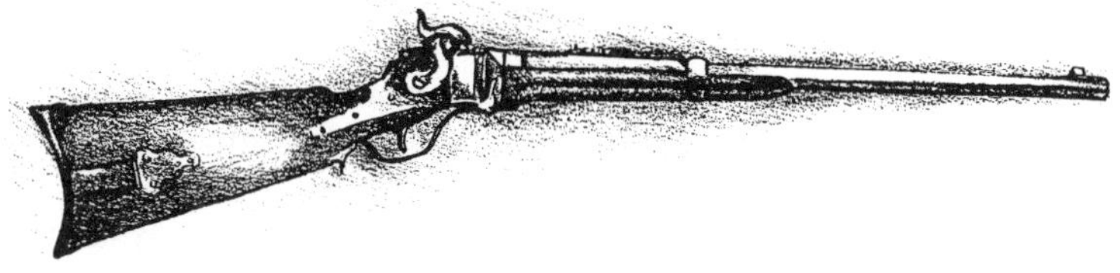

JULY 1862~NOVEMBER 1862

LAFE WILSON

Captain USA

Cynthiana, Kentucky, July 17, 1862

Surrounded by Confederate forces and vastly outnumbered, the Federal soldiers were determined to hold the town of Cynthiana. However, a Confederate battery at Licking Bridge on the outskirts of town took a heavy toll on the small Federal force. Wilson, mortally wounded, lay near the depot. He was heard to say,

"Never surrender, boys."

He continued to fire his revolver until he died. The boys, escaping from the town, did not surrender.

HENRY B. STONE

Lieutenant Colonel, USA

Slaughter Mountain, Virginia, August 9, 1862

In a charge in which only eight company officers were not killed or disabled, Stone of the Fifth Connecticut was mortally wounded and perhaps taken prisoner. His last letter home clearly indicates that he knew the dangers of being a leader in battle.

> "Camp near Culpepper Court House,
> Monday [Saturday], July 26, 1862.
>
> My Dear Wife:
>
> I expect that the time has nearly arrived when we shall have a bloody battle, as I understand to-night that the enemy is crossing the Rapidan river, with twenty-five or thirty thousand men, and advancing towards us. If so, probably before you receive this we shall have fought one of the severest battles of the war. I have to write you what to do if I shall be so unfortunate as to fall on the field of battle. If I am killed, I wish to have Mr. William Montgomery to settle my affairs, pay all of debts, and with the remainder buy a small place for you and the children, where you could live comparatively comfortable with the pension you would receive from the Government.
>
> The children are now older enough to assist you some about the house, and in a few years, if they live, they will be grown to manhood, when I trust they will

not forget they [sic] mother. I have endeavored, so far, to rear them to usefulness, and I cannot but believe that they will be a comfort to you, and an honor to society, living in the fear of God; if they are guided by His holy law, they cannot go astray.

If I should fall, my body will probably be sent home; I shall wish to be laid in the cemetery at Danbury, in a lot selected by my family.

It has been my desire and intention to have Theodore educated as a soldier, at West Point, if it were possible, and if practicable I wish it to be so. He is or will be well calculated for a soldier, having the right temperament and constitution. Melly is active and will succeed any where if rightly directed and watched over. Seymore, the dear little fellow, I hope will outgrow his misfortune, and if possible should have a good education, that will fit him for any kind of business. If I judge rightly, he will acquire knowledge faster than either of the others.

All of them are so constituted that they will be easier and better governed by kindness than by harsh treatment. Every care should be taken in rearing our little girl, as her future happiness depends more upon her disposition and amiableness of character, than that of men; women are more dependent than the other sex.

You must think strange that I write you thus, for it is my duty to you all; and as it could not be done after I am killed, it is quite proper, and justice to you that I should do it now while the opportunity offers.

And now, my dear wife, be of good cheer. If it should please the Lord to take me from you, He has promised to be the widow's God and Father to the Fatherless. His promise are sure! and if we meet no more on earth, I hope to meet you in heaven, where there shall be no more wars, or rumors of war, and the weary are at rest. No man could lose his life in a nobler cause; and although it would be a great pleasure to me to spend the remainder of my life in the midst of my family, and assist in rearing our dear children and prepare them to fight the battle of life, still I should detest myself if I could quietly look on and refrain from lending a helping hand in this our country's emergency. As our Heavenly Father has not supplied with means to assist pecuniarily [sic]. I must use what He has given me-my good right arm!

And now my dear wife, may God in His infinite mercy protect you, and assist you to rear up our dear children in the fear of His Holy name.

My Dear Children:-This may be the last time I shall ever address you, and I wish to give you a little advice, which will be of great benefit to you in your intercourse with your fellow men through life. First of all, obey the will of your Heavenly father; by doing this you will always enjoy His favor. One of His commandments is to honor and obey your parents. I know you all love your kind mother, and would not willfully grieve her, but you will do it many time carelessly, if you do not try to avoid it; therefore be careful at all times to do nothing she would not approve of.

You, Melly, are the oldest, and the youngest ones will naturally look to you for example; be careful what examples you set before them, and always be kind to all. and watch over your brothers and sisters with a careful eye; in this way you can assist your mother very much. You are all very dear to me, and it would be one of the happiest moments in my life if I could see and converse with you a few moments this evening. That my Heavenly Father will grant me that privilege again, is my sincere prayer. Into his hands, my dear children, I commit you all.

With many kisses, I remain your affectionate father,

H. B. Stone"

UNEDUCATED PRIVATE

USA

Cedar Mountain, Virginia, August 9, 1862

Before going into battle, the uneducated private asked a reporter to write a short message for him.

"My dear Mary, we are going into action soon, and I send you my love. Kiss baby, and if I am not killed I will write to you after the fight."

The message was posted along with the list of the dead that included his name.

THOMAS H. HOFFMAN

Private USA

Gainesville, Virginia, August 28, 1862

Wounded in both legs, twenty-year old Hoffman lay by the side of the road as the 76th New York Volunteer Infantry entered the fight. In a lull in the action, Captain Barnard chanced upon Hoffman and spoke to him as the surgeon was attempting to tend to the wounds. Lifting his shaking hand, Hoffman said,

> "Captain, if I ever get over this, won't I give it to them."

Left by the road as the fight continued, Private Hoffman bled to death, possibly in the Confederate camp where some of the wounded were taken.

ALONZO WATSON

Private CSA

Brawner's Farm, Virginia, August 28, 1862

On the eve of the battle of Second Manassas (Bull Run), the two armies faced each other at close range. From behind a rail fence, Watson of the 15th Alabama regiment fired his musket until a minie ball found him. He sank to the ground murmuring,

> "Oh, Lordy, I am a dead man."

SAMUEL GARLAND

Brigadier General CSA

South Mountain, Maryland, September 14, 1862

Assigned to protect Fox's Gap, Garland's forces were pressured and threatened to falter. Garland rode into the action where he met Colonel Ruffin who questioned Garland's presence so close to the action. Garland replied,

> "I may as well be here as yourself."

At that moment both men were hit, Garland receiving a bullet in the back. Dying, he said to his aide,

> "I am killed. Send for the senior colonel."

WILLIAM "BULL" NELSON

General USA

Louisville, Kentucky, September 29, 1862

Unable to co-operate with General Jefferson C. Davis over defense preparations, Nelson quarreled with Davis who, in the company of Governor Morton, confronted Nelson in the lobby of the Galt House. Accused by Davis of taking advantage of his (Nelson's) higher authority, Nelson belligerently said,

"Speak louder, I don't hear you very well."

and after the accusation was repeated,

"I don't know that I did, Sir."

Nelson then slapped Davis saying,

"There, damn you, take that!"

and then turned to Governor Morton and said,

"By God, did you come here also to insult me?"

As Nelson made his way upstairs, he said to a bystander,

"Did you hear the damned insolent scoundrel insult me, sir? I suppose he don't know me, sir. I'll teach him a lesson, sir!"

Upstairs, at the door to General Buell's room, Nelson heard his name called, turned and saw Davis armed with a revolver. He shouted,

"Not another step farther!"

but Davis shot Nelson in the chest. He lingered for a few minutes before dying.

"Send for a clergyman. I wish to be baptized. I have been basely murdered."

JAMES BAKER

Colonel USA

Corinth, Mississippi, October 3, 1862

As the battle at Corinth raged, Baker was shot while charging at the head of his regiment. Lying mortally wounded, his last words were,

"I die content. I have seen my regiment victoriously charging the enemy."

PLEASANT ADAM HACKLEMAN

General USA

Corinth, Mississippi, October 3, 1862

While trying to rally panic-stricken men under heavy fire, Hackleman was mortally wounded. Later that night in Corinth, he died with General Thomas A. Davies in attendance. He told Davies,

"I am dying, but I die for my country. If we are victorious, send my remains home; if not, bury me on the field."

WILLIAM RUFUS TERRILL

Brigadier-General USA

Perryville, Kentucky, October 8, 1862

A Virginian who decided to stay loyal to the Union, Terrill was in his first battle as a general. In mid-afternoon, rallying his men after a Confederate onslaught, Terrill was hit in the breast by shrapnel that destroyed a piece of his left lung. He exclaimed,

> "Major, do you think it's fatal? My poor wife, my poor wife."

Surrounded by aides and officers, he died at 11 p.m.

McPHEETERS

Colonel CSA

Near Thibodeaux, Louisiana, October 27, 1862

A veteran of eight engagements, Colonel McPheeters and the Crescent Regiment fought well, but could make no headway against the Union forces in the Louisiana bayou. Aware that the swamp behind him prevented a quick withdrawal, McPheeters, upon seeing Federal reinforcements arriving, ordered his first retreat. As his men began to move out, he said,

> "We could have fought that first regiment all day, but those other fellows are coming sure."

While calmly watching the withdrawal, he was killed by a bullet in the head.

PETER KELLY

Private USA

Land's Church, Virginia, November 6, 1862

In a small cavalry engagement, Kelly of Company E, 8th New York Cavalry suffered a saber cut from ear to ear. Though several companions came to his aid, he could only utter,

> "Water"

before quickly bleeding to death.

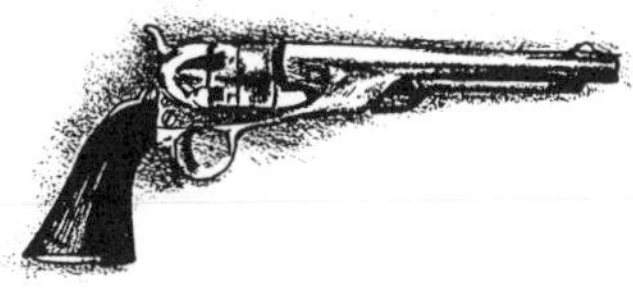

SECOND BATTLE OF BULL RUN (MANASSAS)

PENNSYLVANIA FAMILY MAN

USA

Near Groveton, Virginia, August 29, 1862

On the eve of Bull Run, this soldier, mortally wounded, lay in the woods far from his camp. When a wandering Confederate stumbled over him in the dark, he begged,

"Water, water, for God's sake water!"

After draining the Confederate's canteen, he made another request:

"Now turn me on my back that I may look once more at the beautiful sky and watch the bright stars."

Knowing that death was near, he warned his benefactor,

"Your turn may come next."

After speaking of his family and home in Pennsylvania, he became delirious and murmured,

"How beautiful the heavens are tonight, Emma, and how bright the stars. Come, Eddie, get upon papa's knee."

He died saying,

"My wife...my child..."

MARK KERNS

Artillery Captain, USA

Manassas, Virginia, August 30, 1862

As the Confederates swarmed toward the guns, all the gunners of the 1st Pennsylvania Artillery abandoned their position except for Kerns. As the enemy approached and demanded his surrender, Kerns fired a charge of canister, killing many soldiers. Shot down, with his last breath he made his final point to his enemy:

"I promised to drive you back or die under my guns, and I have kept my word."

PHILIP KEARNY

Major General, USA

Near Manassas Virginia, September 1, 1862

Attempting to gather up scattered troops in order to continue the fight, the brave and daring Kearny rode into a cornfield. In the rain he approached soldiers and questioned,

"What troops are these?"

The answer, "Forty-ninth Georgia," sent Kearny galloping away and, though he hung over the side of his horse, a bullet hit his spine, killing him instantly.

National Archives

Philip Kearny received the wrong answer when he asked, "What troops are these?"

CHARLEY

Captain's son, CSA

Manassas, Virginia, August 30, 1862

After the battle, the wounded sixteen-year old lay on the battlefield in the dark. Between sobs he called for help and was finally found by his father to whom the boy, plagued by wasps, immediately apologized.

> "Father, my leg is broken but I don't want you to think that is what I am crying for. I fell in a yellow-jackets' nest and they have been stinging me ever since. That is what makes me cry. Please pull me out."

He died in his father's arms.

THORNTON F. BRODHEAD

Colonel, USA

Manassas, Virginia, August 31, 1862

Mortally wounded, Colonel Brodhead wrote a final letter to his wife.

> "My Dear Wife:--
>
> I write to you mortally wounded, from the battle-field. We have again been defeated, and ere this reaches you your children will be fatherless. Before I

die let me implore that in some way it may be stated that General Pope has been outwitted, and that McDowell is a traitor. Had they done their duty as I did mine, and had led as I did, the dear old flag had waved in triumph. I wrote to you yesterday morning. To-day is Sunday, and to-day I sink to the green couch of our final rest. I have fought well, my darling; and I was shot in the endeavor to rally our broken battalions. I could have escaped, but would not until all our hope was gone, and was shot,--about the only one of our forces left on the field. Our cause is just, and our generals,--not the enemy's,--have defeated us. In God's good time he will give us the victory.

"And now, good by, wife and children. Bring them up—I know you will—in the fear of God and love for the Saviour. But for you and the dear ones dependent, I should die happy. I know the blow will fall with crushing weight on you. Trust in Him who gave manna in the wilderness.

"Dr. North is with me. It is now after midnight, and I have spent most of the night in sending messages to you. Two bullets have gone through my chest, and directly through my lungs. I suffer little now, but at first the pain was acute. I have won the soldier's name, and am ready to meet now, as I must, the soldier's fate. I hope that from heaven I may see the glorious old flag wave again over the undivided country I have loved so well.

"Farewell, wife and friends, we shall meet again."

National Archives

The quiet flow of Bull Run was interrupted twice as the armies clashed on its banks in two major battles.

BATTLE OF ANTIETAM

National Archives

Jesse Reno led his men gallantly, even with his dying words.

JESSE LEE RENO

Major General, USA

South Mountain, Maryland, September 14, 1862

Advancing toward Sharpsburg, the Federals were confronted by Confederate forces intent on preventing their passage through the ridge known as South Mountain. The "gallant and dashing" Reno led an attack but was cut down by a musket ball. As stretcher-bearers carried him away, he shouted to Samuel Sturgis,

"Sam, I'm dead."

After the battle, General Sturgis, in a General Order to the troops, commended the men for their bravery and stated that Reno's last words were:

"I can be no longer with my men. Let them know that I will be still with them in spirit."

D. S. MILES

Colonel USA

Harper's Ferry, (West) Virginia, September 15, 1862

In the face of a Confederate attack, Miles put up the white flag to surrender Harper's Ferry. However, the shelling continued for another forty-five minutes during which time Miles received a mortal wound. After surrendering, with enemy forces occupying the town, Miles, tended by a surgeon and officers, said to one of them,

"Captain, I have done my duty to my country, and I am ready to die. God bless you."

Later, a court of inquiry censured Miles' hasty surrender.

HUGH W. McNEIL

Colonel USA

Near Sharpsburg, Maryland, September 16, 1862

Leading Pennsylvania regiments across a field in the face of enemy fire from the woods, McNeil and his men were forced to lie down every few paces to avoid the volleys. When McNeil believed they were close enough, he rose up and shouted,

"Forward, Bucktails, forward!"

Though he was instantly killed by a bullet in the chest, his men routed the Confederates.

RICHARD DERBY

Captain USA

Near Sharpsburg, Maryland, September 17, 1862

On the morning of the battle, Derby of the 15th Massachusetts Infantry wrote the following letter:

> Boonesville, Sept. 17th, 1862
>
> We marched from Frederick, and are now encamped near Boonesboro, between that and the Potomac.
>
> There has been some fighting, but we were not engaged. It looks now as though there would be a battle before Stonewall Jackson can get across the river on his retreat.
>
> This is a beautiful country, and we have fared quite comfortably.... We hear very bad news from Harper's Ferry, but get no reliable particulars; yet prospects are bright with us for giving the rebs a good whipping at this point.
>
> Richard Derby.

During the battle he cheered on his men until he was shot in the temple. Placed at the foot of a tree he died without regaining consciousness.

DECAPITATED OFFICER

USA

Near Sharpsburg, Maryland, September 17, 1862

In a battle known for its 540 artillery pieces, just as the Union officer shouted,

"Come on, boys! Let's go get the rebs!"

a cannon ball, travelling at approximately 1,000 mph, severed his head from his body.

WISCONSIN CORPORAL

USA

Near Sharpsburg, Maryland, September 17, 1862

After the fighting in the cornfield, the corporal of the 2nd Wisconsin was found by Lieutenant Haskell who asked if the messy chest wound was caused by a piece of shell. The corporal feebly explained,

> "No, I was wounded first by a musket ball, and afterwards a rebel thrust a bayonet into my breast."

WISCONSIN OFFICER

USA

Near Sharpsburg, Maryland, September 17, 1862

As the Black Hat Brigade made their charge, this young officer, waving his sword, yelled to the Wisconsin boys,

> "Company E! On the right, by file, into line!"

and was shot in his opened mouth.

INDIANA SOLDIER

Private USA

Near Sharpsburg, Maryland, September 17, 1862

When the 27th Indiana regiment charged into battle, this private fell with a terrible wound. Moving to the rear, he sat down, opened his uniform and realized the truth. To a fellow soldier he said,

> "Well, I guess I'm hurt about as bad as I can be. I believe I'll go back and give 'em some more."

LOUIS PUMPHREY

Sergeant CSA

Near Sharpsburg, Maryland, September 17, 1862

While the 3rd Arkansas lay on the field trying to avoid heavy fire, Pumphrey, keeping the men calm and orderly, repeated,

> "Keep close and be brave!"

Though he lay huddled to the earth waiting for the onslaught to slacken, he could not hide from a minie ball that passed through his body.

ELDERLY SOLDIER

Private CSA

Near Sharpsburg, Maryland, September 17, 1862

After Gordon's Brigade attempted to hold the center against a Federal onslaught, a gray-haired man, mortally wounded, lay on the ground beside his dead son. To Gordon, who was passing by, the old soldier said,

> "Here we are. My boy is dead, and I shall go soon. But it is all right."

WALTER PERRY

Officer, CSA

Shepherdstown, (West) Virginia, September 19, 1862

Wounded at Sharpsburg while leading a charge two days earlier, Walter Perry was unable to be moved further than Shepherdstown. While the army retreated, Walter's brother, Frank, remained with him and in a letter recorded some of Walter's comments. When Frank told Walter that death was near, Walter replied,

> "I thought as much, Frank, from the first, as you did not tell me that I would ever get well."

Comparing his future to that of his General's wounded son, Walter said,

> "Mine is indeed sadder than his, as I am cut off in my youth, just as I put out my hand to reach for the prizes which are awarded to the successful."

As his strength waned, he murmured,

> "This is enough to say, don't you think so?"

When Frank tried to talk to him again, Walter, breathing slowly, said,

> "Frank, we have talked that all over and it can't be pleasant to you and it certainly is not pleasant to me. Goodbye, goodbye, goodbye to you all!"

After a long period of silence, Frank asked if Walter still recognized him. Opening his eyes for the last time, Walter breathed,

> "Who, Frank Perry? I think I do, Frank."

BATTLE OF FREDERICKSBURG

REBEL CHEERER

CSA

Near Fredericksburg, Virginia, December 11, 1862

As Federal soldiers built a bridge over the Rappahannock and prepared to cross, this Confederate soldier reined in his horse on the opposite shore and yelled,

"Hurrah for Jeff Davis!" *

A Federal soldier met the challenge by shooting the exuberant Confederate off his horse.

JAMES C. NOON

Lieutenant (Adjutant) USA

Near Fredericksburg, Virginia, December 13, 1862

Having often said that he would die in his first battle, Noon of the 133rd Pennsylvania Infantry left a farewell letter for his brother when, under heavy artillery fire, his regiment approached the river near Fredericksburg. Forced to leave his horse when it was time to cross the pontoon bridge, the six-foot three-inch Noon, convinced that he would not be returning, dismounted and said,

"Goodbye, horse."

Noon was killed early in the action, shot in the temple while urging the men to charge.

EDWIN M. PLATTS

Corporal USA

Fredericksburg, Virginia, December 13, 1862

As he waited to cross the pontoon bridge before going into battle, seventeen-year old Platts of the 5th Massachusetts Battery said to his tent mate,

"Now we are going into a hot place. Look out for yourself."

When his tent mate reciprocated with the same warning, Platts, just recently promoted, replied,

"No man can call me a coward."

A short time later as he entered the battle, he was hit by a musket ball just above the heart.

GEORGE DASHIELL BAYARD

General USA

Fredericksburg, Virginia, December 13, 1862

After briefly penetrating General Jackson's line, the Union troops led by General Bayard were driven back, Bayard receiving a mortal wound. Before dying, he dictated a will in a note to his family:

> "My black mare and sorrel horse I give to you, father. There are about sixty dollars in my pocket-book. There are papers in my trunk to be turned over to the Department (Quartermaster's) to settle. Once more, good bye, beloved father, mother, sisters, all.
>
> Ever yours, George D. Bayard"

CHARLES E. DART

Sergeant USA

Fredericksburg, Virginia, December 13, 1862

Color-bearer for the 14th Connecticut Volunteers, Dart, wounded, fell during the charge up Marye's Heights. As another sergeant stooped to pick up the flag, Dart said,

> "I will take care of it."

He rose to his feet but immediately died.

ARTHUR BUCKMINSTER FULLER

Chaplain USA

Fredericksburg, Virginia. December 13, 1862

Chaplain of the Massachusetts Sixteenth, Fuller had been honorably discharged because of poor health but, knowing a great battle was impending, he volunteered to stay with the regiments. On the streets of Fredericksburg he asked Captain Dunn,

> "Captain, I must do something for my country. What shall I do?"

Dunn posted Fuller in front of a grocery store where he coolly loaded and fired until a sharpshooter killed him, shooting him twice, hitting him in the chest and spine.

JAMES B. PERRY

Captain USA

Fredericksburg, Virginia. December 13, 1862

Mortally wounded in the chest, Perry lay where he fell, cared for by fellow officers. To one of them he said,

"I know I shall not recover from this wound, but I am content if I can see the old flag once more."

Though his sight failed before the flag arrived, he clutched it as he died.

JOHN M. JONES

Captain USA

Fredericksburg, Virginia. December 14, 1862

In the charge made by the 133rd Pennsylvania Infantry on the 13th, Jones of Company F, hit in the arm and thigh, said to another captain,

"I am wounded."

Urged to leave the field, he insisted,

"I shall never leave while my boys are here."

To the boys he exclaimed,

"Be true as steel, my boys!"

After receiving a head wound, he was taken to the field hospital where he died at three in the morning.

FREDRICKSBURG SOLDIER

USA

Fredericksburg, Virginia, December 15, 1862

Wounded on December 13th by a bullet through the brain, he was left behind when Burnside's army deserted Fredericksburg. When spoken to, he simply repeated,

"Captain, captain."

FREDERICKSBURG PRIVATE

USA

Georgetown, District of Columbia, December, 1862

Wounded at Fredericksburg, the soldier was brought to Union Hospital. Nurse Louisa May Alcott, seeing the soldier's untouched meal, offered to feed him. He replied,

"Thank you, ma'am; I don't think I'll ever eat again, for I'm shot in the stomach. But I'd like a drink of water, if you aint too busy."

By the time Nurse Alcott returned with the water, the man had died.

JOHN THE BLACKSMITH

USA

Georgetown, District of Columbia, December, 1862

The thirty-year old Virginian earned the respect of future novelist Louisa May Alcott who nursed him at Union Hospital. He suffered from a lung wound received at Fredericksburg. As he lay dying, his friend, Ned, came to his bedside and, for want of words, merely asked how he was doing. John replied,

"Most through, thank heaven! Take my things home, and tell them that I did my best. Good bye, Ned."

After a parting kiss, John was left to gasp out his remaining moments, at the very end rising from his pillow to cry,

"For God's sake, give me air!"

LEWIE

Private USA

Georgetown, District of Columbia, December 27, 1862

At Union Hospital, the soldier identified only as Lewie was nursed by Louisa May Alcott and Hannah Ropes for ten days before he succumbed to the three bullet wounds he received at Fredericksburg. His last comment was to Nurse Alcott who had given him a drink of water:

"Thank you, madam; I think I must be marching on."

HOSPITAL DEATHS 1861~1863

Of the approximately 630,000 Civil War deaths, perhaps two thirds were the result of diseases. Dysentery, malaria, diarrhea, pneumonia, measles and smallpox were major killers. When the medical resources of the camps were strained, ill soldiers were transferred to city hospitals. Washington, D. C. had over fifty medical facilities, many of them in government buildings such as the Patent Office. Hospitals were also located at Georgetown College, schools, Saint Elizabeth's Insane Asylum and hotels. Richmond, Virginia had hospitals of various sizes at over 170 locations, including churches. Unaware of modern ideas of sanitation, the operators of these facilities could not prevent the many deaths that occurred from blood poisoning, tetanus and gangrene. It has been estimated that the hospitals killed as many men as they saved.

MEASLES PATIENT

Private USA

Washington, D. C., Mid-December, 1861

One of twenty-six members of the 11th Maine who contracted measles, he was one of four who died soon after arriving at Columbian College Hospital. Shortly before he died, he mused,

> "What will my poor mother say when I am laid away from her?"

"SWEET-FACED LITTLE SOLDIER"

Private USA

Washington, D. C., January 4, 1862

Youngest of the patients in Columbian College Hospital, a private in the 11th Maine, he realized he was dying. He told his nurse,

> "If only I could see my dear mother and my little sister Lucy, only once more, I would be happy."

After asking for a Bible reading and prayers, he fell asleep. Upon awakening, he was resigned to his death, having dreamed of Jesus. Bidding good-bye to those around him, he said,

> "Jesus can make a dying bed feel soft as downy pillows are. Good-bye, nurse; I shall met you again in Heaven."

Some minutes before the boy died he uttered,

> "Glory to God in the Highest! I am going home!"

ELEVENTH MAINE PATIENT

Private USA

Washington, D. C., January 7, 1862

The fourth young soldier to die in Columbian College Hospital within three days, he expressed his gratitude to Nurse Pomroy just before dying.

> "You have been the only mother that I have seen since I left home. May God bless you, not only in this world, but in that better world hereafter, for being such a good friend to us poor, sick soldiers. God bless you."

National Archives

Wounded soldiers at the field hospital near Fredericksburg, 1862.

GEORGE SHUE

CSA

Springfield, Missouri, Spring 1862

One of Sterling Price's soldiers, he was captured along with sixteen others. In the hospital at Springfield, he told visitor John McCorkle,

> "John, I am awful sick. I feel very queer. Please tell the doctor to come."

By the time McCorkle returned with the doctor, Shue had died.

LOGAN

CSA

Charlottesville, Virginia, May 24, 1862

As nurse Ada W. Bacot and a minister stood by his bedside, Logan knew the end was near and was "perfectly resigned to the will of God." As the minister prayed, nurse Bacot began to cry. Logan said to her,

"Do not weep for me. I am going to rest. I am perfectly willing to die. I do not suffer as much as you think."

Knowing his mother would be pleased that he died as a Christian, he thanked all those who had aided him. To the minister he praised nurse Bacot:

"She has done for me as if I were her son." *

CHARLEY

USA

Alexandria, Virginia, 1862

As Charley lay in bed, he realized that the stump of his amputated leg had begun to bleed. To a passing orderly he said,

"H___, my leg is bleeding again."

Having experience with bleeding arteries, H___ placed his thumb in the only appropriate place to stop the bleeding, high up on the thigh, and called for the surgeon. When the surgeon realized that the situation was hopeless, the only point of surgery being the spot under the thumb, Charley asked for his brother who soon arrived. For three hours, while H___ maintained the pressure on the artery, Charley made his final arrangements with his brother. When he was finished, he said,

"Now, H___, I guess you had better remove your thumb."

When H___ protested, Charley continued,

"But it must be done, you know. I thank you very much for your kindness, and now, good-bye."

Charley turned away as H___ removed his thumb. Three minutes later he was dead.

JOHN C. CALHOUN VEITCH

Private, CSA

S. C. Hospital, Manchester, ? July 6, 1862

Wounded in the breast at Gaines's Mill on June 27th, Veitch passed on his last message to fellow soldier and friend Berry Benson. The final words were directed to Veitch's sister.

"Give her my love, and tell her I died for my country."

IRRATIONAL SOLDIER

Hammond General Hospital, Washington, D. C.

As with many of the soldiers suffering fever, he spoke irrationally until death claimed him, his last words containing more significance than his delirious mind knew:

"Mother, you are wanted."

BEWILDERED SOLDIER

Hammond General Hospital, Washington, D. C.

Lying in bed, the chaplain by his side performing the sad duty of the deathwatch, he said, as death approached and his senses left him,

> "The room is growing dark. Are they putting out the lights?"

W. J.

Hammond General Hospital, Washington, D. C.

To the hospital chaplain he dictated his final message:

> "Write to my wife and tell her before this reaches her I shall be no more. I rest on Jesus and on Him alone. I see His blood. Tell her to let my bones lie here. *I* shall be in Heaven. I leave her and the children in God's hands."

W. O.

Hammond General Hospital, Washington, D. C.

Suffering from chronic diarrhea, the killer of many soldiers, he used the services of the chaplain to send a final word home:

> "Write to my father just how I am. Don't conceal anything."

In gratitude to the chaplain he said,

> "I am giving you a great deal of trouble but it strengthens me to have you here."

Asked by the chaplain if he had hope of salvation in Christ, he responded,

> "I can do nothing else."

WILLIAM McC

Hammond General Hospital, Washington, D. C.

Near death, and expressing no wish to recover, the religious soldier requested of the chaplain,

> "Write to my father and tell him I am very ill, that my whole trust is in Jesus."

Later, he added,

> "I want my family to know that religion has sustained and comforted me."

Dying, he said,

> "Jesus, I am coming."

D

Color-Sergeant

Hammond General Hospital, Washington, D. C.

Having suffered a severe shoulder wound that repeatedly hemorrhaged, he knew that death was approaching. To the chaplain he said,

> "Tell my mother I die in a good cause. I have carried the flag over the land of the brave and the free. Don't let those traitors run away with the country! Don't let them destroy the country! They should not as long as I could stand on my feet."

When the chaplain gave thanks to God, the dying man responded,

> "Yes, He conquers for me. I look to Christ for pardon."

National Archives

Patients at Carver Hospital, Washington, D. C.

T. D.

Hammond General Hospital, Washington, D. C.

Suffering from fever, speechless, T. D. died leaving a small red morocco notebook in which was a picture of Mary back home in Wisconsin. The water-damaged notebook contained a couplet:

"Not a sigh shall tell my story,
Silent death shall be my glory."

Following were some notes on his last days in the army:

> "Moved camp for the third time and went to digging. Another hot day—I am sick. July 14th—We are getting our pay to-day; I say we, but I am not getting any—digging wears out so many clothes. 16th—Another hot day; I am sick; I am hardly able to do anything. We are here in the old camp again. Have had no letter for three weeks. On the march—sleeping out of doors. Lay in the rain all night—sick—don't know where I shall go. Marched again—lay out of doors—very wet—no shelter."

ILLINOIS SOLDIER

USA

Nashville, Tennessee, 1862

Going out in style, the dying soldier inspired the other patients in the hospital in the Cherry Street Church by often singing his favorite song, *Rally Round the Flag, Boys!* He was singing with his final breath:

"Rally, boys, rally once again..."

WILLIAM H. KELLER

Private USA

Bladenburg, Maryland, December 14, 1862

Desperately ill for a week with typhoid fever, twenty-one year old Keller was cared for in his tent by two friends. In his last moments near midnight he asked to be turned over and given a drink. Weakly he said,

"I aint dead yet. I was *almost* gone."

A little later he uttered his last words:

"My Jesus, O my Jesus."

LIBBY PRISON

Libby Prison, located in Richmond, Virginia, consisted of three large tenement buildings, each four stories high. Before the war the west building had been leased by Captain Luther Libby who ran his business under the sign L. LIBBY & SON, SHIP CHANDLERS & GROCERS. After the battle of First Manassas or Bull Run, the army commandeered Libby's building for use as a hospital and prison. The army acted with such haste that the sign was left untouched and the prison became known as Libby Prison. Over 50,000 Federal prisoners entered the prison during the course of the war.

PALE YOUNG MAN

USA

Richmond, Virginia, July 14, 1862

This prisoner of war had the opportunity to speak to a Federal clergyman/doctor who was allowed to visit the prisoners. On the night he died the pale young man told his visitor,

> "Many of [my] nights were wakeful, and in this place all [my] life came back to [me]; and it was strange, [I know] it must be mere illusion, but [I] heard at times the church bells of [my] native village, and sometimes heard the congregation sing, at other times the tones of the organ, and stranger than all, [I] several times heard [my] father and mother call [me] as when [I] was a child." *

EUGEN (?) M. (?) DEMMING

Captain, USA

Richmond, Virginia, July 17, 1862

Wounded and captured near Savage Station on June 30th, Captain Demming of the 61st New York began to weaken after two days in Libby Prison. This cultivated man grasped the doctor's hand and said,

> "I wish you to stay by me, my friend, for I am greatly troubled. Pray for me that I may do nothing wrong."

As death overtook him, he became delirious:

> "Do not detain me now. I see my wife across the street; she stands at the door and beckons me. Excuse me; I must go to her."

JOHN C. WARBURTON

USA

Richmond, Virginia, July 17, 1862

After losing a leg at the battle of Glendale, Warburton of the 5th Pennsylvania Reserves was captured and held in Libby Prison where he contracted tetanus. On the day he died he made a will, dictated a message to his mother and, after committing himself to Christ in the presence of the clergyman, he said,

"Now all is done. I have nothing to do but die."

He suffered greatly and died during the night.

DIARIST

USA

Richmond, Virginia, July 17, 1862

Having kept a diary of camp scenes and battles up to the day of the battle of Mechanicsville, the Diarist, probably wounded, made only one more entry after being incarcerated at Libby Prison:

> "Libby Prison, July____:--As you would receive the blessing of a dying soldier send this to my brother in Canonsburgh, Pennsylvania."

National Archives

Libby Prison, Richmond, Virginia

DECEMBER 1862~APRIL 1863

ILLINOIS SUFFERER

USA

Prairie Grove, Arkansas, December 7, 1862

During an attack on Confederate forces on Prairie Grove Ridge, the 37th Illinois met fierce resistance and, after twenty minutes, reluctantly retreated. Left behind with many other wounded soldiers, one huge Illinois man, his thigh shattered by a minie ball, waited in great pain. When a Confederate soldier approached, the Illinois man, pleaded,

> "For the love of God, friend, kill me and put me beyond such intolerable misery."

After confirming the dying man's seriousness, the Confederate asked if he could have the Illinois soldier's canteen and overcoat. The man replied,

> "Yes, yes. Everything."

After being told to shut his eyes, hold his breath and that it would be over in a minute, the Illinois soldier was released from his suffering.

ELBRIDGE GRAVES

Private USA

Kinston, North Carolina, December 14, 1862

Twenty-four years old, Graves was a member of the 45th Massachusetts Volunteer Militia known as the Cadet Regiment. When the regiment was sent to North Carolina, Graves wrote home conveying the attitude of the eager cadets who had not yet seen battle:

> "We are never tired of cheering for the glorious old flag under which we are fighting."

As the soldiers built a camp and defenses, Graves optimistically commented on the countryside:

> "[T]he soil was honest, and the trees were all loyal, and were making great sacrifices for freedom."

Finally encountering the enemy, Graves, during a lull in the battle, suggested to his comrades that they sing a hymn. Graves and the others sang,

> "Ye Christian heroes, go proclaim
> Salvation in Emanuel's name."

Moments after concluding the hymn, Graves was killed, shot in the shoulder, the ball veering down to his groin.

MISSISSIPPI PRIVATE

CSA

Murfreesboro, Tennessee, December 31, 1862 (?)

Having fallen against a fence with two bullets in his breast, the young soldier gasped out his dying words to General Jones and his staff who had stopped to see if the boy wanted water.

> "No...I don't want anything. Tell the boys—I'm dying, but if...they are short...of cartridges...my cartridge box...is full."

"TENNESSEE BOY"

Private CSA

East Tennessee, January, 1863

Wounded at the battle at Stones River around New Year's Day, the young Confederate died with his sixteen-year old brother and his mother at his bedside. Even as he died he tried to comfort his distraught family:

> "Mother, goodbye. And you, Tom, goodbye. Be of good heart, mother. God will take care of you, and save—save the—"

DROWNING SOLDIER

USA

Forsyth, Missouri, March 1, 1863

After one boatload of troops crossed the stream safely by ferry, a second boatload suffered an accident, spilling men and mules into the icy water. As men on shore watched helplessly, the hapless victims were swept downstream. One soldier came within a few feet of the shore and cried out,

"Oh, can't you save me?" *

Arms numb from the cold, he slipped below the surface of the water.

JOHN W. PULLER

Major CSA

Kelly's Ford, Virginia, March 17, 1863

As the 5th Virginia prepared to meet the advancing enemy, Puller jokingly shouted to a friend,

"Harry, leave me your haversack if you get killed!"

Somewhat later, in the thick of battle, bent over his horse's neck and ignoring the fighting, he heard Colonel Rosser frantically ask him why he was not rallying the men. Puller, shot in the chest, explained,

"Colonel, I'm killed."

EDGAR A. KIMBALL

Lieutenant Colonel, USA

Fort Nansemond, Virginia, April 12, 1863

About 2 a.m., Lieutenant Edgar A. Kimball, perhaps intoxicated, intervened to support a sentry who was not receiving the countersign from brigadier commander Corcoran:

> "That's right, sentry. Let no one pass without the countersign."

Kimball ordered Corcoran, whom he apparently did not recognize, to halt. When Corcoran demanded identification, Kimball's reply was,

> "It is none of your God damned business!"

Kimball repeated this line several times after each request for identification. Then drawing his sword, Kimball declared,

> "You cannot pass here."

When the general identified himself, Kimball shouted,

> "I do not care a damn who you are!"

To Corcoran's request to move out of the way, Kimball said,

> "Not for no damned Irish son of a bitch like you or anyone else."

When Kimball, waving his sword, advanced, Corcoran drew a pistol and fired, the bullet striking Kimball in the neck, severing the carotid artery. Kimball, having fallen, quickly arose, and advanced, challenging Corcoran to

> "Fire again!"

but he collapsed and expired.

WALTER C. WYKER

Private USA

Near Eagleville, Tennessee, April 22, 1863

While on picket duty on the Shelbyville Pike, Wyker of Co. K accidentally shot himself. To the soldiers gathered around him he passed on his last message:

> "Tell my mother I died a true soldier."

DUNCAN McVICAR

Lieutenant-Colonel, USA

Near Spotsylvania, Virginia, April 30, 1863

Ordered to find the enemy, McVicar took his 6th New York cavalry to within three miles of Spotsylvania. Here, by moonlight, he clashed with Jeb Stuart's soldiers. Sensing a trap, McVicar shouted the order,

> "Sixth New York, follow me! Charge!"

In the cavalry charge he received a bullet in the heart.

GUERILLAS & BUSHWHACKERS

REBEL BUSHWHACKER

Near Winchester, Virginia, April 15, 1863

Tracked down and captured by Federal soldiers in search of bushwhackers who had ambushed and killed two cavalrymen, the Bushwhacker refused to surrender his weapons and, when told that he would be shot, pointed to his head and replied:

"There are my brains. Shoot, and be damned!"

The soldiers shot him in the stomach and finished him off with two bullets to the head.

JIM VAUGHAN

Guerilla

Fort Leavenworth, Kansas, May 29, 1863

One of Quantrill's associates, Vaughan was captured and hanged. On the day he died he made a statement that offered other guerillas justification for revenge and murder:

> "You may kill me, but you'll never conquer me, and taking my life today will cost you a hundred lives and this debt my friends will pay in a short time."

SCOTT

Guerilla Captain

Westport, Missouri, June 17, 1863

In retaliation for the hanging of Jim Vaughan on May 29th, a guerilla band attacked Federal soldiers. As he rode into the action, Captain Scott was shot in the neck. He threw up his hands, shouted,

"I am a dead man"

and fell from his horse.

WILLIAM BLEDSOE

Guerilla

Baxter Springs, Kansas, October 6, 1863

Spotting two hundred Federal soldiers and nineteen wagons, one of which was a bandwagon carrying the band, a large group of guerillas gave pursuit. Shot by a member of the band, Bledsoe fell from his horse. To fellow guerilla Fletch Taylor, who stopped to aid him, Bledsoe said,

"Fletch, that outfit have shot and killed me. Take my two pistols and kill all of them."

In the chase that followed, the bandwagon lost a wheel and the stranded band members were easily killed by the guerillas.

GEORGE TODD

Guerilla Captain

Independence, Missouri, October 21, 1864

Shot through the neck by a Federal sniper at Independence, he died an hour later. In delirium his mind wandered to an earlier fight.

"Boys, we're in a tight place. Where is John McCorkle? If he was here he could get us out of this."

CHAMP FERGUSON

Guerilla Leader

Nashville, Tennessee, October 20, 1865

After waging guerilla warfare for four years, Ferguson surrendered in 1865, believing that if he took the oath of allegiance he would be released. However, he was tried for murder and other acts violating the rules of war and sentenced to hang. A short time before his death he explained,

"We were having a sort of miscellaneous war up there, through Fentress County, Tennessee, Clinton County, Kentucky, and all through that region. Every man was in danger of his life; if I hadn't killed my neighbor he would have killed me. Each of us had from twenty to fifty proscribed enemies, and it was regarded as legitimate to kill them at any time, at any place, under any circumstances, even if they were wounded or on a sick-bed."

The forty-four year old fighter remained calm on the scaffold. His main concern in his gallows speech was that,

"[my] body should not be given to the doctors to be cut up." *

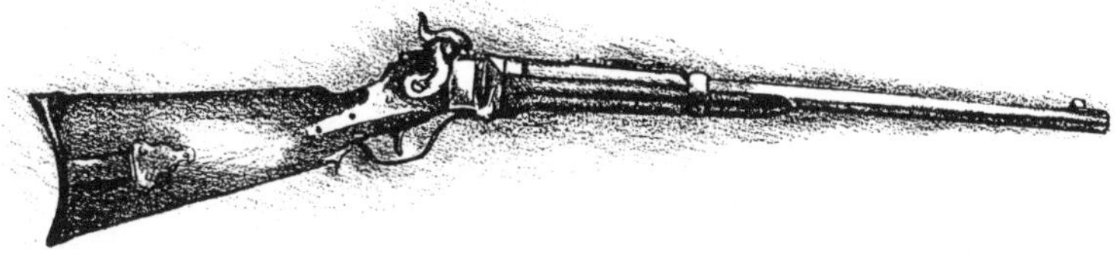

THE LAWRENCE, KANSAS MASSACRE

A large band of guerillas descended on the town of Lawrence, near the Kansas-Missouri border. The town had suffered in the past for its anti-slavery sentiments. The raiders, led by William Clarke Quantrill, were bent on killing all the males old enough to carry a gun. In the hours of murder and destruction, approximately one hundred and fifty civilians were murdered, eighty-two women widowed, and two hundred and fifty children orphaned.

GEORGE W. BELL

County Clerk

Lawrence, Kansas, August 21, 1863

From his hillside home on the outskirts of the town, Bell saw the rebels gather. Taking his musket and cartridge box, he headed for main street, telling his family,

"They may kill me, but they cannot kill the principals
I fight for. If they take Lawrence, they must do it over
my dead body."

Since the rebels were in the main street by the time Bell arrived, he moved to the back streets, finding other citizens. He asked them,

"Where shall we meet?"

Informed that the situation was hopeless, Bell abandoned his rifle and hid in a house where he was discovered by one of the guerillas, a former acquaintance who promised him safety. Trusting the man, Bell came out and was executed in the street.

LOUIS CARPENTER

Judge

Lawrence, Kansas, August 21, 1863

Though several bands of raiders had robbed him earlier in the day, he was not harmed until another gang arrived. When one of the guerillas asked the young Judge where he was from, the Judge responded,

"New York."

The Judge's answer did not sit well with the pro-slavery guerillas who immediately shot him. Though wounded, he escaped into his house but was eventually driven out and shot again, the final bullet fired into the Judge's head while his wife, in an effort to protect him, covered him with her body.

Kansas Images
Josiah C. Trask mistakenly thought that Quantrill's raiders could be appeased by co-operation.

JOSIAH C. TRASK
Editor
Lawrence, Kansas, August 21, 1863

When the guerillas surrounded the home of Dr. Griswold, Trask and three other eminent citizens and their wives were assured they would not be harmed and that, if they quietly surrendered, the town might be saved. Trask, editor of the *State Journal,* led the way, saying,

"If it will help save the town, let us go."

Outside, the four men were escorted a short ways down the street and then unceremoniously shot.

MAY 1863~JUNE 1863

ALABAMA SOLDIER

CSA

Bank's Ford, Virginia, May 4, 1863

After the battle, the wounded Alabama soldier was found by two Federal soldiers who were wandering the battlefield. As the soldiers approached, the wounded man asked,

"Will you do me a favor?"

Upon receiving their assurance, he gave them his personal possessions and letters and an address to which to send them. Then shaking hands with the Federal soldiers he said to one of them,

"You are probably the last man I shall have a chance to speak to."

Then he watched his "enemies" depart, carrying with them his last messages to his loved ones.

National Archives

Stonewall Jackson's last words provided a fitting end for the legendary hero.

THOMAS JONATHAN "STONEWALL" JACKSON

Lieutenant-General CSA

Guiney's Station, Virginia, May 10, 1863

After his stunning victory on May 2nd, thirty-nine year old Jackson and his officers had ridden to the front and, in the darkening twilight, he was shot three times, probably by his own troops who did not recognize him. In great pain he was taken to a nearby field hospital where a doctor informed him that his left arm had to be amputated two inches below the shoulder. Jackson said,

> "Yes, certainly, Dr. McGuire. Do for me whatever you think best."

As the chloroform took effect, he lost consciousness murmuring,

> "What an infinite blessing."

Two days later, Dr. McGuire received orders to move Jackson away from the enemy to Guiney's Station. Jackson told the doctor,

> "If the enemy does come, I am not afraid of them; I have always been kind to their wounded, and I am sure they will be kind to me."

During the following week at a house at Guiney's Station he contracted pneumonia. When his wife and child arrived, he said to her,

> "I know you would gladly give your life for me, but I am perfectly resigned. Do not be sad. I hope I may yet recover. Pray for me, but always remember in your prayers to use the petition, Thy will be done."

The day before he died, he said to Dr. McGuire,

> "I see from the number of physicians that you think my condition dangerous, but I thank God, if it is His will, that I am ready to go."

The next morning, told that his recovery was doubtful, Jackson responded,

> "It will be infinite gain to be translated to Heaven."

Then he encouraged his wife to return to her father:

> "You have a kind and good father, but there is no one so kind and good as your Heavenly Father."

When she told him that he would die before sundown, he replied,

> "Oh, no; you are frightened, my child; death is not so near; I may yet get well."

Informed that there was no hope, Jackson asked his doctor:

> "Doctor, Anna says you have told her that I am to die today. Is it true?

Hearing the doctor's confirmation, he responded,

> "Very good, very good. It is all right."

Later that afternoon, told that the army was praying for him, Jackson said,

> "Thank God, they are very kind. It is the Lord's day. My wish is fulfilled. I have always wanted to die on Sunday."

His doctor offered him brandy and water but Jackson refused, saying,

> "It will only delay my departure, and do no good. I want to preserve my mind, if possible, to the last."

However, as the time passed, he became delirious, saying shortly before his death,

> "Order A. P. Hill to prepare for action! Pass the infantry to the front! Tell Major Hawks..."

His last words were,

> "Let us cross over the river, and rest under the shade of the trees."

His body was taken to Richmond and then to Lexington where he was buried.

ALABAMA CONFEDERATE

CSA

Champion's Hill, Mississippi, May 16, 1863

After the battle of Champion's Hill which saw fierce hand to hand combat, the fifty-year old Confederate lay mortally wounded on the battlefield. Seeing a small group of Federal soldiers riding near him, he lifted himself up on his elbow and inquired,

> "For God's sake, gentlemen, is there a Mason among you?"

Before being left on the field to die, he gave to one of the Federal soldiers, a fellow Mason, a piece of jewelry to be sent to his wife in Alabama.

"FINE-LOOKING CONFEDERATE"

CSA

Clinton, Mississippi, May 17, 1863

Wounded at the battle of Champion's Hill, this soldier, probably an officer, was taken to Grant's headquarters, a little cottage at Clinton. Near midnight, the man, blinded by a shot that severed his optic nerves, shouted,

> "Kill me! Will someone kill me? I am in such anguish that it will be mercy to do it. I have got to die! Kill me! Don't let me suffer!"

He died before morning.

JAMES McDANIELS

Private CSA

Near Monticello, Kentucky, Late May, 1863

When the 9th Tennessee and various Kentucky regiments came upon a thousand Union soldiers in a place called Horse

Shoe bottom on Greasy Creek, McDaniels had a leg shot off by a shell. Seeing the blood spurt, he cried,

"I will die!"

Though given aid almost immediately, he died from loss of blood.

JACK CARTER

Private, CSA

Near Monticello, Kentucky, Late May, 1863

As the Union soldiers took cover in heavy woods, Carter and his comrades lay in an open field exchanging shots with the enemy. Seeing an opportunity, Carter arose and, aiming from a kneeling position, declared,

"I'll get that yank behind that tree."

Unfortunately, a Union marksman was quicker, shooting Jack in the head.

JACOB KENT LANGHORNE

CSA

Brandy Station, Virginia, June 9, 1863

Eight days before he was killed, the Virginia Military Institute cadet, full of enthusiasm, was looking forward to being a soldier in the 2nd Virginia cavalry.

> "Camp Near Culpeper CH
> June 1st 63
>
> Dear Papa
>
> I received your letter a day or two ago and have commenced to answer it once or twice but was interrupted. I had my mare valued at 650$. My arms have not cost me a cent. One of the men gave me a rifle captured at Chancellorsville and I drew a pair of pistols from ordnance wagon which I will return as soon as I can capture one. I bought a saber for 3$, the best one I have seen. Capt Steptoe sends his regards to you. He has just ordered us to strike tents and I have to close. Let me know when Jimmy Langhorne is coming. Love to all, I remain your attached son, Kent.
>
> Send me some stamps. J Kent."

BENJAMIN F. DAVIS

Colonel USA

Beverly Ford, Virginia, June 9, 1863

Although he held the rank of acting Brigadier General in the Eighth Illinois Cavalry, Davis moved into the thick of the action waving his saber to rally his men. Just after saying,

"Come on, Eighth, follow me!"

a Confederate soldier fired three revolver shots at him, the third hitting Davis in the head.

PHILIP GRUB

Corporal USA

Liberty Gap, Tennessee, June 25, 1863

Minutes before victory was achieved, Grub was hit, saying to a companion who comforted him,

"Have I not always done my duty?"

"JESSE SCOUT"

USA

Near Winchester, Virginia, June 9(?), 1863

While riding down a narrow lane, the Jessie Scout, one of a group of Union scouts who dressed in Confederate uniforms, met a Confederate cavalryman who had taken the precaution of wearing a white handkerchief around his neck, the badge by which the Jessies identified each other. Though he drew his pistol, the Jessie Scout was deceived by the casual familiarity of the approaching cavalryman. As they neared each other, the Jessie Scout inquired,

"Where are you going?"

Though the response sounded convincing, the Jessie Scout further questioned the man about his company. Told that they belonged to the same group, the Jessie Scout said,

"Why, I don't remember seeing you, though I haven't been detailed long myself."

When the man mentioned the 12th Pennsylvania, the Jessie Scout, convinced of the man's authenticity, put away his pistol. Then, distracted by the man's query about the handcuffs looped on the Jessie Scout's saddle, he bent over to obtain them and explained,

"There is a Reb out at old Griffith's, and I am going after him."

Put completely off guard, the Jesse Scout was easily sabered through the body. He fell off his horse and died within five minutes, his last words acknowledging his enemy's smooth deception:

"You sold me pretty well, but I don't blame you."

BATTLE OF CHANCELLORSVILLE

ROBERT REILY

Colonel USA

Chancellorsville, Virginia, May 3(?), 1863

Facing superior numbers and heavy firing on May 2, Colonel Reily and his men of the 75th Ohio held their position as long as possible, then retreated. Wounded in the leg, Reily, was taken to the field hospital where his leg was amputated. He died soon after the operation. Some of his soldiers noted that shortly before his death he said,

> "I am proud of the 75th. They done their duty, and did not leave until they were ordered."

National Archives

Hiram G. Berry, unafraid of danger, left the front lines only after being mortally wounded.

HIRAM GREGORY BERRY

Major General, USA

Chancellorsville, Virginia, May 3, 1863

An efficient and reliable soldier, Berry often bypassed messengers and delivered his orders in person. As he prepared to meet an assault he rode out to organize a brigade and was shot, possibly by a sharpshooter.

To an attendant he said,

> "I am dying. Carry me to the rear."

VERMONT SOLDIER

Private, USA

Chancellorsville, Virginia, May 3, 1863

Shot in the jugular vein and obviously dying, this young member of the 2nd Vermont Volunteers was asked if he wanted any last words conveyed to his friends. He managed to say,

"Tell them that I was a good soldier."

ELISHA FRANKLIN "BULL" PAXTON

General, CSA

Chancellorsville, Virginia, May 3, 1863

Rowdy when young, Paxton, who had a premonition of his death the previous evening, constantly consulted his pocket Bible. During the battle in which he commanded the Stonewall Brigade, Paxton fell, his final words indicating that he was unaware that he had been shot in the chest.

"Tie up my arm."

ABANDONED SOLDIER

Private, USA

Chancellorsville, Virginia, May 3, 1863

Abandoned by his comrades who took the time to make a shelter for him by hooking his India-rubber blanket to several muskets, the private lay as if dead until a Confederate soldier, seeking booty, started to remove the blanket. Then he opened his eyes and informed the looter,

"I ain't dead yet."

The Confederate soldier apologized and moved on without taking the blanket.

YOUNG SOLDIER

Private CSA

Chancellorsville, Virginia, May 3, 1863

After the Confederates had driven the Federal forces back at a heavy cost, the young soldier, his usual good humor and enthusiasm now fading as he leaned against a tree, clutched his wounded side and told a passing officer,

"Major, I am dying, and I shall never see my regiment again, but I ask you to tell my comrades that the Yankees have killed but not conquered me."

"YOUNG FELLOW IN GRAY"

Private CSA

Chancellorsville, Virginia, May 3, 1863

Exploding shells ignited the dry grass and leaves on part of the battlefield. Wounded soldiers, both blue and gray, were unable to escape the path of the flames. As able soldiers from both armies worked side by side trying to save the wounded from the fire, a "young fellow in gray" watched in horror as the fierce flames fueled by pine pitch and rosin roared around him. As the flames engulfed him, he shrieked,

"O Mother! O God!"

HENRY WEST

Corporal USA

Chancellorsville, Virginia, May 3(?), 1864

Shot through the thigh, the bone shattered, young West, perhaps bleeding to death, was taken to the field hospital in the rear. Optimistically, he declared,

"I guess that old Joe West's son has lost a leg."

National Archives

RETALIATION EXECUTIONS

Picked at random from the inmates at Gratiot Street Prison in St. Louis, six Confederate prisoners were sentenced to be shot by firing squad, apparently in retaliation for the deaths of seven Federal soldiers killed near Union, Missouri. Three thousand people witnessed the execution.

CHARLES MINNEKIN

Private CSA

St. Louis, Missouri, October 29, 1864

At the time of the execution, after the men were tied to posts, Minnekin was allowed to make a statement to the crowd. Though he spoke for himself, his words can also be interpreted as the last words of the five men who died with him:

> "Soldiers, and all of you who hear me, take warning from me. I have been a Confederate soldier four years and have served my country faithfully. I am now to be shot for what other men have done, that I had no hand in, and know nothing about. I never was a guerilla, and I am sorry to be shot for what I had nothing to do with, and what I am not guilty of. When I took a prisoner I always treated him kindly and never harmed a man after he surrendered. I hope God will take me to His bosom when I am dead. Oh Lord, be with me."

As the sergeant put a blindfold on him, Minniken said,

> "Sergeant, I don't blame you. I hope we will meet in heaven."

Then he spoke to the firing squad members:

> "Boys, when you kill me, kill me dead."

He then said good-bye to his comrades.

Private **George T. Bunch** and Private **James W. Gates**, also tied and blindfolded, joined in the farewells, saying,

> "Boys, farewell to you all, and the lord have mercy on our poor souls."

JOHN A. NICHOLS

Private CSA

St. Louis, Missouri, October 29, 1864

At the time of execution, Nichols, one of the six men condemned to be shot, asked if a postponement was possible. Told he must die, he shed tears and said,

"O, to think of the news that will go to father and mother"

and he repeated,

"Lord, have mercy on my poor soul."

HARVEY H. BLACKBURN

Private CSA

St. Louis, Missouri, October 29, 1864

After being blindfolded, Blackburn said goodbye to his fellows tied to the posts at the execution scene in St. Louis. Thirty-six soldiers fired their rifles, and Blackburn, fatally shot, cried out,

"Oh, kill me quick!"

ASA LADD

Private CSA

St. Louis, Missouri, October 29, 1864

One of the six men executed at Gratiot Prison, Ladd wrote two letters before the execution:

"St. Louis, Mo,
Oct. 29, 1864

Dear Wife & Children:

I take my pen with trembling hand to inform you that I have to be shot between 2 & 4 o'clock this evening. I have but few hours to remain in this unfriendly world. There is 6 of us sentenced to die in retaliation of 6 union soldiers that was shot by Reeves men. My dear wife don't grieve after me. I want you to meet me in Heaven. I want you to teach the children piety, so that they may meet me at the right hand of God. I can't tell you my feelings but YOU can form some idea of my feeling when you hear of my fate.

I don't want you to let this bear on your mind anymore than you can help, for you are now left to take care of my dear children. Tell them to remember their dear father. I want you to go back to the old place and try to make a support for you and the children. I want you to tell all my friends that I have gone home to rest. I want you to go to Mr. Conner and tell him to assist you in winding up your business. If he is not there get Mr. Cleveland. If you don't get this letter before St. Francis River gets up you had better stay there until you can make a crop, and you can go in the dry season. It is now half past 4 AM. I must bring my letter to a close, leaving you in the hands of God. I send you my best love and respect in the hour of death. Kiss all the children for me. You need have no uneasiness about my future state, for my faith is well founded and I fear no evil. God is my refuge and hiding place.

Good-by Amy.
Asey Ladd"

The second letter was written to his father, Ransom Ladd:

"Gratiot Street Prison

St. Louis, Mo. Oct. 29th, 1864

My Dear

Father, I am condemned to be shot today between the hours of two & four o'clock p.m. in retaliation for some men shot by Reeves (Major Wilson and six men). I am an innocent man and it is hard to die for an others sins. You can imagine my feelings when I think of you my wife & children. I want my family to come back to my old place. If you live till peace is made I want you to settle up and pay off all my debts. You need have no uneasiness as to my future state for my faith is well founded and I fear no evil, God is my refuge and hiding place. Meet me in Heaven.

Good bye"

Ransom Ladd outlived his son by only eleven months, dying in September, 1865.

CIVILIANS

WILLIAM B. MUMFORD

Confederate Citizen

New Orleans, Louisiana, June 7, 1862

Before the Federal army took possession of New Orleans, Mumford took down the United States flag at the Mint and walked the streets with a piece of the flag in his buttonhole. After the Federal army moved in, Mumford was arrested and publicly hanged before a crowd of thousands. On the gallows he said,

> "I consider that the manner of my death will be no disgrace to my wife and child; my country will honor them."

DR. JOHN ADAMS

Principal

September 28, 1862, Andover, Maryland

In his last journal entry, the Principal of Phillips Academy wrote:

> "This day I enter my ninety-first year. The year just closed has been one of trial and deep solicitude. My country! oh my country! I do not expect to see peace restored during the short remainder of my stay, but I am earnestly looking forward to that everlasting rest which remaineth to the people of God. God reigns. He will accomplish His purposes. Amen and Amen."

JAMES WARFIELD

Blacksmith/ Farmer

Near Olathe, Kansas, October, 1862

Suspected of pro-Union sympathies, Warfield was taken from his home at midnight by bushwhackers, possibly Quantrill's men who on this night also killed a Mrs. Styles for being a Union spy. Forced to accompany the rowdy gang, Warfield said,

> "Let me get my hat and coat."

Told he would not need them, he was taken down the road, followed by his wife and daughter. In the dark, some distance from the house, perhaps encouraged by his captors, he turned to the two females and said,

"Mother, you's better go back. I don't think Billie will hurt me and if he does, you couldn't do me any good."

Later a shot was heard. Warfield's body was found by his daughter in the road the next morning.

OBADIAH SMITH

Near Spring River, Missouri, Spring 1863

When Quantrill and his men arrived, dressed in blue overcoats, Smith was drawn into conversation. As Quantrill admired Smith's rifle, Smith made the mistake of saying,

"Yes, and I've turned many a damned rebel over with it."

Quantrill tried to kill Smith but Smith ran, only to be shot down by one of Quantrill's men.

"COLONEL" WITHERS

Civilian

Near Jackson, Mississippi, July 11, 1863

After the fall of Vicksburg, Federal forces confronted Confederate forces on the land of Colonel Withers. As the battle began, the seventy-year old gentleman took the gun and cartridge box of a dead Confederate and began shooting at the blue uniformed "invaders." While the Confederate soldiers would lie down to reload, Withers remained standing until hit. He fell, rounding out his life with a final statement:

"There, they've got me."

ROSALIE BEEKMAN

Civilian

Natchez, Mississippi, September 3, 1862

Fleeing with her family during the naval bombardment of Natchez by the Union gunboat *Essex*, seven-year old Rosalie fell, mortally wounded. When her father yelled to her to get up, she cried,

"I can't, papa; I'm killed."

With blood flowing from her wounds, she was carried to shelter but died some hours later.

EXECUTIONS

Most military executions were performed on deserters. As the war dragged on, desertion on both sides became a problem for military leaders. The deserters were usually men who had been away from home too long, men who had joined the army as substitutes for others who had been drafted, men who had joined for the bounty money or men who were merely tired of war. In the early, desperate part of the war, desertion was not tolerated and the firing squad spectacle was used as a warning to the other soldiers. Later in the war death sentences were often commuted.

Men were also executed, usually hanged, for crimes such as murder, and for spying.

ROWLAND

Deserter CSA

Corinth, Mississippi, May, 1862

Considered a deserter because he had quit the Confederate army and later joined the Union army, Rowland was captured at Shiloh, court-martialled and sentenced to be shot. As he was being taken out to be executed, he observed that the grave that had been dug for him had filled with rain. Rowland said to the man bailing out the water,

> "Please hand me a drink of that water, as I want to drink out of my own grave, so the boys will talk about it when I am dead, and remember Rowland."

After asking for a second drink because he had heard that

> "water was very scarce in hell,"

he cursed the Southern generals and said he would show the rebels

> "how a Union man could die."

Apparently he made the following speech:

> "Fellow soldiers, Tennesseeans—I was forced into Southern service against my will, and against my conscience. I told them I would desert the first opportunity I found, and I did it. I was always a Union man and never denied it, and I joined the Union army to do all the damage I could to the Confederates. I believe the Union cause is right and will triumph. They can kill me but once, and I am not afraid to die in a good cause. My only request is that you let my wife and family know that I died in supporting my principles. My brothers there would shoot me if they had a chance, but I forgive them.

> Now, shoot me through the heart that I may die instantly."

He removed his hat, coat and necktie, laid his hand on his heart and said,

"Aim here."

ASA LEWIS

Corporal 6th Kentucky, CSA

Murfreesboro, Tennessee, December 26, 1862

Hearing of the death of his father and his mother's need of him, Lewis requested a furlough. Continually denied, Lewis twice left his regiment without permission. Captured and brought back for the second time, he was sentenced to be shot for desertion. With the entire division witnessing the execution, Lewis made his final remarks to the execution squad:

> "Comrades, I know you are all grieved to do this work, but don't be distressed. None of you will know who kills me for you know one of your guns has no ball in it. Each man may think his was the harmless gun. But I beg of you to aim to kill when the command 'Fire' is given. It will be merciful to me. Good-bye."

WRIGHT

Private CSA

Shelbyville, Tennessee, January, 1863

Only seventeen or eighteen years old, Wright was sentenced to death by firing squad. After silently watching for two hours the preparations for his execution, he was placed at the post. Upon the firing of the muskets, he cried out,

"O, O, God!"

YANKEE SPY

Chattanooga, Tennessee, Summer, 1863

As the sixteen-year old boy accused of spying was taken to the gallows, his fourteen-year old companion, also doomed to hang, began to beg and plead. The sixteen-year old Spy gave the younger boy a slight kick and said,

"Be a man!"

WILLIAM MINIX

Private, USA

Murfreesboro, Tennessee, June 16, 1863

Having left his unit nine months earlier when it was in Kentucky, twenty-five year old Minix was sentenced to be shot by firing squad. Two days before his execution he wrote to Colonel Thomas J. Cram:

> "...as you are doubtless aware I am sentenced to be shot on Tuesday next — others have also been sentenced the same as my selfe who have done much worse then my selfe and yet have been reprieve and I feel shure if you would intrest your selfe on my behalfe my life might be saved and I will promase no swear if I escape that awful degrading death I will hence forth be a true and loyal and a law abiding soldier may God help me for I cannot – help my selfe"

FRANCIS SCOTT

Private, USA

New Orleans, Louisiana, August 14, 1863

Thirty-year old Scott was sentenced to be shot for murder. Before the execution he made the following statement:

> "Fellow Soldiers:
>
> I am about to die for killing Major Bullen. I did kill him, and would do the same thing over under similar circumstances.
>
> I had never met him before that day. My company had come down from Port Hudson to Donaldsonville, and we stopped there in the fort. That evening Major Bullen came to the breastworks and told my captain he must remain on the breastworks, as he was going to withdraw his detachment. The captain told him we were under marching orders, and he did not think it right he should be left there. The Major replied: 'You must obey orders, sir, and I order you to remain here.'
>
> Without intending anything wrong, I happened to say, 'Well, captain, we'll take care of these breastworks, and protect the nine months' men from the enemy.' At which the Major turned upon me, and some words passed between us, when he drew his revolver and aimed it at me.

My musket was at the order, and I brought it to the ready, and before he could fire I fired at him. I shot him through the wrist and in the body.

I killed him and am content to die for it. Had he killed me there would have been nothing done. An officer is never punished for killing a soldier. I hold no malice against anyone, and freely forgive everybody, as I hope all will forgive me. Had General Banks a thousand men like me, they would be worth more than all the conscripts that the State of Maine can send into the field."

He then dropped to his knees and said,

"I am ready."

Two of the seven bullets that hit him struck his heart.

JOHN SMITH

Private, USA

Second Army Corps Headquarters, Virginia, August 29, 1863

After fighting at Fredericksburg, thirty-seven year old Smith deserted along with many others. Re-enlisting as a substitute under an alias, he was soon recognized by former comrades, arrested and sentenced to be shot. Just before being executed along with another deserter, he shook hands with the officer in charge, then raised his hands to the sky and twice cried out,

"Oh, God, have mercy upon us!"

GEORGE BLOWERS

Private, USA

Near Brandy Station, Virginia, December 18, 1863

Sentenced to death for deserting, Blowers and John Tague faced a firing squad as the entire Division stood by, forced to witness the event. After the shooting, Tague died instantly but Blowers fell, struggled for a few moments and uttered,

"Oh dear me!"

WINSLOW N. ALLEN

Private, USA

Kellys Ford, Virginia, December 18, 1863

After deserting from his company, Allen, a year and a half later, rejoined the army for the three hundred dollar bounty. Unfortunately, he was assigned to his former company and was immediately recognized as a deserter. On the day of his execution, the twenty-four year old Allen said to his captain:

"Captain, you have been kind to me, which I can only return by my prayers for your welfare. Take this [his pocket-book]. It is all I have, and when I am gone, please lay this [a prayer written on a card] on my breast."

Accompanied to the firing squad by the Captain, Allen replied to the Captain's request for some last word for his family.

"No, only tell them I love them all!"

DAVID OWEN DODD

Spy CSA

Little Rock, Arkansas, January 8, 1864

Dodd was caught while he attempted to get by the picket guards without a pass. A search revealed incriminating papers. He was court-martialled, found guilty of spying and executed by hanging.

"Military Prison Little Rock
Jan. 8th. 1 oclock am 1864

My Dear Parents and Sisters

I was arrested as a Spy and Tried and Sentenced to Be Hung to Day at 3 o'clock. The time is fast approaching But thank God I am Prepared to Die I Expect to meet you all in Heaven. Do not weep for me for I will be better off in Heaven. I will Soon Be out of this World of Sorrow and Trouble. I would like to See you all Before I Die But let God's will Be Done, not Ours. I Pray to God to give you Strength to Bear your Troubles while in this World. I Hope God will Receive you in Heaven--there I will meet you. Mother I Know it will Be Hard for you to give up your only Son But you must Remember that it is God's will. Good Bye. God will give you Strength to Bear your Troubles. I Pray that we may meet in Heaven.

Good Bye. God Bless you all.
Your Son and Brother
David O. Dodd

Standing in the prison wagon, the noose around his neck fastened to a crossbeam, Dodd told the executioner who forgot to bring a blindfold,

"You will find a handkerchief in my coat pocket."

With the wagon removed, Dodd strangled to death, his toes touching the ground.

WILLIAM E. ORMSLEY

Private, USA

Vienna, Virginia, February 7, 1864

Twenty-year old Ormsley deserted and joined the enemy. Captured shortly thereafter, he was court-martialed on February 6th and sentenced to be shot the next day. Obtaining permission to speak to the assembled troops, he said:

> "Comrades: I want to acknowledge that I am guilty and that my punishment is just. But I want also that you should know that I did not desert because I lost faith in our cause. I believe we are on the right side, and I think it will succeed. But take warning from my example, and whatever comes do not desert the old flag for which I am proud to die."

HENRY MILLER

Private USA

Jacksonville, Florida, April 16, 1864

Only five years in America, German born Miller enlisted as a substitute and, with several others, tried to desert. Captured past the last guard station with all his belongings, he was brought back to camp, given a quick trial and executed. Asked by the chaplain if he had any message for his friends, Miller stated,

> "I have no friends, want no prayers and have no favors to ask of anybody." *

THOMAS R. DAWSON

Private, USA

Morrisville, Virginia, April 24, 1864

The Englishman Thomas Dawson, a Crimean War veteran, winner of the Victoria Cross and Cross of Honor, left camp with two other soldiers. The men drank, became intoxicated and were accused of rape. Dawson faced a court-martial for desertion and rape and was sentenced to be hanged. On the gallows he made a final statement:

> "You may break my neck, but you won't break the seal of manhood."

After the drop, his feet touched the ground and a desperate executioner had to manually jerk the condemned man into the air.

BATTLE OF GETTYSBURG

WILLIAM KELLY

Private USA

Gettysburg, Pennsylvania, July 1, 1863

After four color-bearers of the 24th Michigan Volunteers had been shot down, Kelly took the flag from his Colonel to whom he said,

"You shall not carry the flag while I am alive!"

Moments later he too was killed, shot in the heart.

National Archives

John Reynolds fought desperately to give Union troops time to arrive at the Gettysburg battlefield.

JOHN FULTON REYNOLDS

General USA

Gettysburg, Pennsylvania, July 1, 1863

When the Confederate soldiers threatened to take the high ground, Reynolds gathered his inadequate forces and shouted,

"Forward, forward, men! Drive those fellows out of that! Forward! For God's sake, forward!"

As he urged them onward, a Confederate sharpshooter put a half-inch hole behind Reynold's right ear. Reynolds fell from his horse, gasped, and died with a slight smile on his face.

STEPHEN C. WHITEHOUSE

Captain USA

Gettysburg, Pennsylvania, July 1, 1863

As the 16th Maine formed for battle, Whitehouse said to another officer,

"Adjutant, I wish I felt as brave and cool as the colonel appears."

When the order to fall in came, he tersely said,

"Good-bye, Adjutant. This is my last fight."

The advancing regiment quickly came under fire and Whitehouse was killed.

EVANS

Sergeant USA

Gettysburg, Pennsylvania, July 1, 1863

Spotting a flag-waving Confederate color bearer, Evans of the 88th Pennsylvania raised his musket and said to his companion,

"John, I will give those colors a whack."

Before he could fire, a bullet thudded into him. He slowly lowered his musket and fell to the ground.

ASA BLANCHARD

Sergeant-Major USA

Gettysburg, Pennsylvania, July 1, 1863

After three color-bearers of the Nineteenth Indiana fell, Blanchard picked up the flag, waved it and shouted,

"Rally, boys!"

Shot almost immediately, he told the soldiers who stopped to carry him off the field,

"Don't stop for me. Don't let them have the flag. Tell mother I never faltered."

He lived long enough to see his departing comrades save the flag from the advancing Confederates.

ISAAC E. AVERY

Colonel CSA

Gettysburg, Pennsylvania, July 2, 1863

Commanding Hoke's North Carolina brigade, Avery led his men against a much larger force and was mortally wounded. As he lay dying, he wrote his last words on a scrap of paper.

"Tell father that I died with my face to the enemy."

JAMES CROMWELL

Major, USA

Gettysburg, Pennsylvania, July 2, 1863

As attacking Confederates threatened to capture the guns above the Devil's Den, Cromwell of the Orange Blossoms led a charge that appeared to force the Confederates into retreat. His cry of victory was cut short by a bullet that killed him instantly.

"The day is ours!"

AUGUSTUS VAN HORNE ELLIS

Colonel, USA

Gettysburg, Pennsylvania, July 2, 1863

Seeing Cromwell fall, Ellis of the 124th New York regiment rallied his men to try to meet the on-coming Confederates. Swinging his sword, he rose up in his stirrups shouting,

"My God! My God, men! Your major's down; save him! Save him!"

A bullet in the forehead tumbled him from his saddle.

STEELE

Sergeant USA

Gettysburg, Pennsylvania, July 2, 1863

During the fierce fighting to protect Little Round Top, Steele was shot, the bullet making a large hole in his chest. He staggered toward his captain and said,

"I am going, captain."

Still on his feet and supported by the captain, he died.

PATRICK H. "PADDY" O'RORKE

Colonel USA

Gettysburg, Pennsylvania, July 2, 1863

In the defense of Little Round Top, O'Rorke of the 140th New York Regiment led two companies to meet the enemy. When they came within forty feet of the Confederates, O'Rorke waved his sword, turned around and said,

"Here they are, men! Commence firing!"

Struck immediately in the neck by a bullet, O'Rorke fell on the rocky slope.

HENRY C. BRAINARD

Captain CSA

Gettysburg, Pennsylvania, July 2, 1863

As the Fifteenth Alabama attacked Little Round Top, Captain Brainard was one of the first men to fall. Before drawing his last breath, he said simply,

"O God, that I could see my mother!"

GEORGE WASHINGTON BUCK

Sergeant USA

Gettysburg, Pennsylvania, July 2, 1863

Buck, who had unjustly lost his rank of sergeant in winter camp, was shot in the breast defending Little Round Top. Found on the field by Colonel Joshua Chamberlain, Buck was only concerned that his contribution be recognized. He whispered,

"Tell my mother I did not die a coward!"

On the spot, Chamberlain, who knew the circumstances of the man's demotion, gave him a battlefield promotion to sergeant.

STEPHEN HINSDALE WEED

Brigadier General, USA

Gettysburg, Pennsylvania, July 2, 1863

Arriving at Little Round Top near the end of the battle, Weed was hit in the spine by a minie ball. Taken off the field to a private residence, he told an aide who had expressed hope for Weed's recovery,

"I'm as dead a man as Julius Caesar."

Later, a Gettysburg girl who stayed by him asked him if he was seriously wounded. He replied,

"Yes, pretty badly."

And was he suffering?

"Yes, I do now, but I hope in the morning I will be better."

Responding to her desire to help him, he made one request:

"Will you promise me to come back in the morning to see me?"

As she was leaving, he reminded her,

"Now, don't forget your promise."

When she returned in the morning, he was dead.

EDWARD E. CROSS

Colonel USA

Gettysburg, Pennsylvania, July 2, 1863

Despite sensing his impending death, the old Indian fighter, Cross, black handkerchief around his head, led his reinforcements into the battle at the Wheatfield. Mortally wounded in the fight, he died later in the evening, consoling himself with his belief that he had led well.

> "I did hope I would live to see peace and our country restored....I think the boys will miss me."

JOHN STEVENS

Private CSA

Gettysburg, Pennsylvania, July 2, 1863

Mortally wounded in the advance on the Wheatfield, Stevens of Georgia refused to quit, saying to his Captain as they neared a fence,

> "Captain, if you will help me over the fence, I will try to go on."

Unable to continue, he lay down for the last time.

SAMUEL KOSCIUZKO ZOOK

Brigadier General USA

Gettysburg, Pennsylvania, July 2, 1863

Leading still more reinforcements into the Wheatfield, Zook was fatally wounded after he led his men over the retreating, and prone, Federal soldiers who were impeding his path to the battle.

> "If you can't get out of the way, lie down and we will march over you!"

National Archives

Samuel K. Zook tolerated no hesitation as he went to his death leading his men into the Wheatfield.

WILLIAM BARKSDALE

Brigadier General CSA

Gettysburg, Pennsylvania, July 2, 1863

The impatient and aggressive Barksdale led his 13th Mississippi regiment in a glorious charge into the Peach Orchard. The terrific assault was eventually stymied and the enraged Barksdale fell, riddled by bullets. Later that night he died despite the efforts of a Federal surgeon to whom Barksdale spoke his last words:

"Tell my wife I am shot, but we fought like hell."

N. E. GRANGER

Lieutenant USA

Gettysburg, Pennsylvania, July 2, 1863

Returning early from an unexpired leave of absence in order to go into battle with his regiment, twenty-six year old Granger of the 111th New York Volunteers wrote, on the eve of his death, a letter, part of which read:

> "You may be anxious to know my feelings. I have made up my mind to be prepared for any event. I trust in God, and in Him I place my hope, knowing that He doeth all things well. Good-bye!"

Shot in the right breast, he was taken from the field. A few friends gathered and, knowing that Granger was dying, asked him for a last message to send home. Just before dying at sunset, he met everyone's expectations by saying,

"Tell them I die for my country."

A. W. PROSEUS

Lieutenant USA

Gettysburg, Pennsylvania, July 2, 1863

Despite his illness, twenty-eight year old Proseus left his sick bed to lead his men into battle. He was killed just after telling his men of the 111th New York Volunteers,

"Stand firm! Don't yield an inch!"

RUBE FRANKS

CSA

Gettysburg, Pennsylvania, July 2, 1863

As the Fourth Alabama impatiently advanced into the enemy fire, Franks in a new, brightly colored uniform gleefully urged his companions to advance quicker than a nearby Texas regiment. As he sought glory, he was perhaps unaware that his bright uniform was an attractive target for the enemy. Surging forward, he shouted,

"Come on, boys; come on! The Fifth Texas will get there before the Fourth! Come on, boys; come on!"

Moments later, a Yankee bullet found him.

JOSEPH WASDEN

Lieutenant Colonel CSA

Gettysburg, Pennsylvania, July 2, 1863

After three hours of battle, as the 22nd Georgia Infantry lay in line of battle near sundown, Wasden, their Lieutenant Colonel was hit in the back by grapeshot. Giving his sword and pistol to the captain, he gave directions that the items should be sent to his wife with the message that he had brought no disgrace on his weapons. After suffering a short time, he uttered his last words:

"Oh, God, is it possible that I must die?"

"FAIR COMPLECTED YOUTH"

Private CSA

Gettysburg, Pennsylvania, July 3, 1863

Because John Kimble had repeatedly missed a Federal soldier who was firing at retreating Confederates after the failed assault on Cemetery Hill, Kimble asked the Youth who was lying beside him to try and hit the man. The Youth of Armistead's Virginia Brigade responded,

"Why, damn him, I have shot at him four times."

Seeing the approaching Federal reinforcements, the boy, having had enough of battle for the day, said,

"I am going out of here."

As he turned to run, a bullet struck him in the head.

JERE GAGE

Private CSA

Gettysburg, Pennsylvania, July 3, 1863

While waiting for Pickett's Charge to begin, Gage of the 11th Mississippi was the victim of a bursting shell that ripped open his stomach and nearly severed his left arm. At the field hospital, he was asked by a surgeon if he had any last words before the opium was administered. Brought to an anguished awareness Gage said,

"My mother, O, my darling mother! How could I have forgotten you?"

With a friend's help, Gage wrote a note, pressed it to his wound and finished with the line:

"This letter is stained with my blood."

JAMES K. MARSHALL

Colonel CSA

Gettysburg, Pennsylvania, July 3, 1863

As part of Pickett's Charge, Marshall had a moment's conversation on the battlefield with Captain Stockton Heth to whom he said,

"We do not know which of us will be the next to fall."

In the midst of the charge on Cemetery Hill, while cheering on his men as they passed the stone fence, he was struck in the forehead by two musket balls.

EDWARD KETCHAM

Lieutenant USA

Gettysburg, Pennsylvania, July 3, 1863

As Pickett's Charge commenced, one of the waiting Union infantrymen was Ketcham, a Quaker, who became the first man in his regiment to fall. Edward's brother, John, witnessed his brother's death. John wrote: "The ball struck him in the temple, and went through his head. He put up his hand, and said,

'Oh!'

and fell on his elbow, quite dead."

WILLIAM MONTE

Private CSA

Gettysburg, Pennsylvania, July 3, 1863

Just before Pickett's Charge began to falter, Monte of the 9th Virginia, viewing the panorama of war, said,

"This is a sublime sight!"

Checking his watch, he added,

"We have been just nineteen minutes coming."

A fragment of shell rushed him into eternity.

LEWIS ADDISON ARMISTEAD

Brigadier General CSA

Gettysburg, Pennsylvania, July 5, 1863

During the famous Pickett's Charge, Armistead, waving a black cap on the end of his sword, led his men toward the Union artillery guns. He shouted,

"Come on, boys! Give them the cold steel!"

Just as he came close enough to put a hand on one of the guns he was mortally wounded. He lingered for several days. Shortly before his death, he sent a message to the enemy commander, his former friend and military companion, General Winfield Scott Hancock.

"Tell Hancock I have done him and my country a great injustice which I shall never cease to regret."

CHARLES R. MUDGE

Lieutenant Colonel USA

Gettysburg, Pennsylvania, July 3, 1863

Mudge of the Second Massachusetts Infantry, ordered to lead a charge into the heavy fighting on the right, summed up his chances with the grim comment:

"It is murder, but it is the order."

He was killed in the charge when his regiment was caught in a burst of enemy fire from its flank.

ALFRED GARDNER

Private USA

Gettysburg, Pennsylvania, July 3, 1863

When the Federal artillery came under fire, many men were killed by enemy shells and their own exploding ammunition chests. As Brown's Rhode Island battery attempted to reload, the gun received a hit, the terrific explosion blasting off one soldier's head. Private Gardner's left arm was severed and he died joyously.

"Glory to God! I am happy! Hallelujah!"

ALONZO CUSHING

Lieutenant USA

Gettysburg, Pennsylvania, July 3, 1863

On the last day of the Gettysburg battles, artilleryman Cushing tried to ignore his fatal wound, leaning against his cannon. Wanting desperately to continue his part of the fight, his last words were to his general.

"I will give them one more shot, sir."

ALLAN

Gunner CSA

Gettysburg, Pennsylvania, July 3, 1863

Having gone through many battles struggling for spiritual understanding, Allan, aided by discussions with Major Robert Stiles, finally found spiritual peace. In his last written communication home he wrote:

> "In the hurry of the march I have little time for thought, but whenever my eternal interests do occur to me, I feel entire assurance of full and free pardon through Jesus Christ, and if called upon to die this moment I think I could do so cheerfully."

As the final battle died away, a shell landed near two artillery pieces, shattering the sponge-staff. When Allen stooped to unkey the other sponge, a percussion shell struck the wheel, the explosion transforming Allan into a "mangled mass."

WILL JENKINS

Private CSA

Gettysburg, Pennsylvania, July 4, 1863

Shot through the body, Will Jenkins of the 7th North Carolina (?) was among the wounded that lay in a grove awaiting medical aid. A Union officer asked if he wanted anything.

> "Only a drink of water. I'm cold, so cold. Won't you cover me up?"

He then asked the officer to write to his family:

> "Tell them all about it, won't you? Father's name is Robert Jenkins. My name is Will."

After some moments of delirium, he died.

"HANDSOME VIRGINIAN"

Private CSA

Gettysburg, Pennsylvania, July 4, 1863

Mortally wounded in Pickett's Charge, he lay calmly with the other wounded. When a Union officer inquired about his wound, he pointed feebly to his chest. Asked if he were afraid to die, the young man whispered,

> "No, I'm glad I'm through."

After a moment of pain, he looked intensely at the officer and said,

> "I'm going home. Good-bye."

YOUNG GETTYSBURG SOLDIER

Gettysburg Field Hospital, Pennsylvania, July 5(?), 1863

Suffering from his wounds, the young soldier refused to complain. At night he whispered to another wounded man,

> "Good night, Lieutenant; I think that I shall go up before morning."

He went to sleep for the last time.

GREENLY

Private USA

Gettysburg, Pennsylvania, July (?), 1863

One of the many wounded left in the makeshift hospital after the battles, young Greenly finally suffered an amputation from which he quickly succumbed, his mother at his bedside.

"Mother—Dear Mother! Good bye! Good—Mother!"

JOHN ALVA OATES

Lieutenant CSA

Near Gettysburg, Pennsylvania, July 25, 1863

Shot eight times in the fighting at Little Round Top on July 2, twenty-seven year old Oates was captured after the Confederate retreat and taken several miles to the Second Division's field hospital. After receiving medical aid, he was nursed for twenty-three days by several women who treated him with kindness. Shortly before he died, he asked them to sing a hymn for him. Then, together, they recited the Lord's Prayer. Moments before he died, he said,

"Tell my folks at home that I died in the arms of friends."

National Archives

Many young men spoke their last words before suffering an amputation at field hospitals such as this one at Gettysburg.

DRAFT RIOTS

DRAFT PROTESTORS

New York, New York, July 14, 1863

Reacting to the drafting of northern soldiers, many white laborers of New York City, fearful that free Negroes would provide cheaper labor in the north, rioted for four days. On Pitt Street, the police fired on the mob killing eight of the crowd who had been roaming the city looting and fighting. The signs they carried read,

"No Draft."

WILLIAM HENRY NICHOLS

Civilian

New York, New York, July 17, 1863

Being black, Nichols and his mother were attacked on July 15th in his home by a stone-throwing mob during the Draft Riots. Fleeing first to the basement, then the back yard, Nichols tried to rescue his mother when the mob caught her as she attempted to climb the fence. He exclaimed,

"Save my mother, if you kill me!"

Seized and beaten with a crowbar, he died two days later in the hospital.

WILLIAMS

Civilian

New York, New York, July 17(?), 1863

During the Draft Riots, Williams, a black man, was attacked on the street on July 14th and severely stabbed and beaten. Rescued by police, he was taken to New York Hospital, where, responding to a request for his identity, he was only able to say:

"Williams."

Without any further communication, he died a few days later.

JULY 1863~APRIL 1864

ALVAH B. PAGE

Gunner USA

Vicksburg, Mississippi, July 3, 1863

Under a flag of truce, artilleryman Page sat calmly on the number two gun while Confederate General Bowen and Colonel Montgomery were taken blindfolded to General Grant's headquarters. As all the guns fell silent, Page, referring to the generals, said,

"I guess they are gone up."

At that moment, a Confederate sharpshooter ignoring the flag of truce, fired a bullet that struck the unguarded Page in the left ear, killing him instantly.

BARTHOLOMEW BURKE

Private USA

Bardstown, Kentucky, July 5, 1863

In the attack by General Morgan on the Federal troops surrounded in Bardstown, young Burke of the 4th U. S. Cavalry, seeking approval even at the moment of sacrifice, shouted to his commanding officer,

"Lieutenant, did I fall like a soldier?"

REBEL PRISONER

CSA

Vicksburg, Mississippi, July 8, 1863

After the capture of Vicksburg, though some of the 32,000 prisoners accepted parole, many of the captives chose to remain as prisoners. One defiant Confederate, refusing to co-operate with his captors, called a guard a

"Damned Yankee son of a bitch!"

With the butt of his rifle, the guard smashed the prisoner in the head.

MARTIN STAMBAUGH

Lieutenant USA

Fort Wagner, South Carolina, July 11, 1863

As the 76th Pennsylvania Infantry assaulted Fort Wagner, the troops attacked in close column, surging forward until they were stopped by a twenty-foot wide water-filled ditch and a blast of grapeshot. As men began to fall, Stambaugh shouted,

"The order is to fall back!"

He died immediately, shot in the head. The men retreated.

NIMROD A. UNDERWOOD

Private CSA

Near Iuka, Mississippi, July 12, 1863

After a raid on Glendale, Mississippi, the Fourth Alabama Cavalry tried to escape with their booty of Federal clothing and stock. Followed by a Federal regiment, Underwood and his companions were forced into a skirmish near Iuka on July 8th. Underwood was shot above the hipbone, the ball lodging above the other hipbone. Taken to a sympathetic home, he died four days later with his mother at his bedside. Knowing death was near, he told her,

"I am going for a good cause. Carry me home to bury me."

CORMANY'S BUDDY

Private USA

Near Shepherdstown, West Virginia, July 16, 1863

In the woods during the Battle of Shepherdstown, Samuel Cormany and his "Buddy" were caught in a cross-fire. Shot in the breast, Buddy dropped, only having a moment to say,

"Oh, I am shot—tell my mother—"

before death claimed him.

SANFORD B. PALMER

Lieutenant USA

Fort Wagner, South Carolina, July 18, 1863

During a charge on Fort Wagner, Palmer of the 10th Connecticut suffered a bayonet wound in his foot. When an officer questioned the seriousness of the wound, Palmer replied,

"It is a very painful wound, but it will not disable me."

He continued to fight until a bullet struck him in the head.

HALDIMAND S. PUTNAM

Colonel USA

Fort Wagner, South Carolina, July 18, 1863

Putnam led the men of Putnam's Brigade in the evening attack on Fort Wagner and, as with the many troops before them, they were pinned down before they could reach the walls. Unlike other commanders, Putnam refused to retreat, begging his men,

"Hold on for a minute, brave men. Our reinforcements are coming!"

Instantly, he was shot in the head and killed, his men being forced to retreat.

JOHN M. OLIVER

Captain CSA

Wytheville, Virginia, July 18, 1863

In the streets of Wytheville, seeing his company surrendering to the Federals, Captain Oliver stood upon a cannon and, swinging his sword above his head, announced that he would surrender only to an officer. After his surrender, as he was being escorted down the street, he was hit in the chest by a minie ball. Falling he said,

"I am killed."

With his final words he gave directions to his Orderly-Sergeant:

"Take this ring from my finger and send it to my sister. And my watch--send it to my mother."

ROBERT RICHARDSON

Private CSA

Near Culpeper Court House, Virginia, August 2, 1863

Suffering with typhoid fever, Robert was taken from camp to the home of George Marshall, his last word a response to his brother's question as to where he felt pain:

"Nowhere."

ROBERT J. SIMMONS

Sergeant USA

Charleston, South Carolina, August 23, 1863.

A month before he died in a Charleston prison, Simmons was involved in the attack on Fort Wagner during which he was captured. On that day he wrote a letter to a family member.

"July 18, 1863.

We are on the march to Fort Wagner, to storm it. We have just completed our successful retreat from James Island; we fought a desperate battle there Thursday morning. Three companies of us, B, H, and K, were out on picket about a good mile in advance of the regiment. We were attacked early in the morning. Our company was in the reserve, when the outposts were attacked by rebel infantry and cavalry. I was sent out by our Captain in command of a squad of men to support the left flank. The bullets fairly rained around us; when I got there the poor fellows were falling down around me, with pitiful groans. Our pickets only numbered about 250 men, attacked by about 900. It is supposed by the line of battle in the distance, that they were supported by reserve of 3,000 men. We had to fire and retreat toward our own encampment. One poor Sergeant of ours was shot down along side of me; several others were wounded near me.

God has protected me through this, my first fiery, leaden trial, and I do give Him the glory, and render my praises unto His holy name. My poor friend Vogelsang is shot through the lungs; his case is critical, but the doctor says he may probably live. His company suffered very much. Poor good and brave Sergeant Wilson of his company, after killing four rebels with his bayonet, was shot through the head by the fifth one. Poor fellow! May his noble spirit rest in peace. The General has complimented the Colonel on the galantry and bravery of his regiment."

SILAS KENT

Lieutenant USA

Bayou Fordoche, Louisiana, September 29, 1863

Caught in a surprise attack on Sterling's Plantation, the men of the 19th Iowa Infantry fought desperately against overwhelming odds. Finally forced to surrender, many of them showed resistance until their rifles were taken out of their hands. During these desperate moments when a soldier did not know if his enemy would fire or surrender, Lieutenant Kent was wounded and fell. At the mercy of his captors, he was shot again. As he lay dying, he told a companion,

"They murdered me after I was down."

ULRIC DAHLGREN

Colonel USA

Near Richmond, Virginia, March 1, 1864

After having been led astray by an informer, twenty-one year old Dahlgren and his cavalry arrived near Richmond too late to attempt their planned raid. As he and his men tried to retreat in the dark, they were ambushed. Dahlgren was shot four times after uttering his challenge:

"Surrender, you damned rebels, or I'll shoot you!"

ROBERT HALL

Private USA

Fort Pillow, Tennessee, April 12, 1864

One of three hundred black soldiers defending Fort Pillow against General Forrest's aggressive men, Hall was sick in the hospital when the attack occurred. The day before he was killed in his hospital bed, he had a surgeon write a letter to his wife:

> "Dear mammy,
>
> I am very sick here in the hospital, but am better than I was, and hope to get well soon. They have been very kind to me, and I find it very sweet to suffer for the dear flag that give me shelter. You must not worry on my account. Tell katy she must not forget to say her prayers and to study her lessons carefully now while she has an opportunity. And, mammy, take good care of the baby; I dreamed of her last night, and I think how sad it would be to die and never see her little face again. But then chaplain says it will be all right in heaven, and he knows better than we do. And, mammy, don't forget we are free now; teach both the darlings to be worthy of their estate."

The three hundred black soldiers were killed in the assault, most of them after the fort was surrendered.

GEORGE THROOP

Lieutenant USA

Near Mansfield, Louisiana, April 8, 1864

Mortally wounded, artillery Lieutenant Throop urged his companions to leave him and make the necessary retreat. Unwilling to leave Throop, young Hugh Wilson put the officer in an ambulance and attempted to find safety. An impassable stream halted their flight. Obviously dying, Throop told Wilson,

> "Hugh, you must go! You will be taken prisoner. I am beyond the reach of the enemy; they cannot harm me. Put something under my head, and then go. Save yourself! Quick, Hugh!"

After placing his jacket under Throop's head, Wilson escaped.

SIMEON BEVERELY

Private USA

Boston, Massachusetts, April 24, 1864

Returning half an hour late from a day-long furlough, the intoxicated and belligerent Beverely of the 12th Maine, upon being stopped by the guard, seized the guard's musket. When the lieutenant on duty pointed his revolver at him, Beverely shouted,

"God damn you! I can lick you!"

Attempting to grab the lieutenant, Beverely was shot above the left eye.

WILLIAM READ SCURRY

General CSA

Jenkins' Ferry, Arkansas, April 30, 1864

At the battle of Jenkins' Ferry, near Camden, the forty-two year old General, though wounded, refused to be taken from the field while the battle was in progress. After two hours, during which time his wound was not attended to, he saw his men retake the field. He inquired,

"Have we whipped them?"

Informed that his men had won, he considered his duty done and, accepting his fate, he told his aides,

"Take me to a house where I can be made comfortable and die easy."

BATTLE OF CHICKAMAUGA

ROBERT STOUT

Private CSA

Chickamauga, Georgia, September, 1863

In camp at ration time, Bob Stout had a presentiment of his death and became serious. Asked if he were ill, he told his friend Sam Watkins,

> "No. Boys, my days are numbered; my time has come. In three days from today, I will be lying right yonder on that hillside a corpse. Ah, you may laugh; my time has come. I've got a twenty dollar gold piece in my pocket that I've carried through the war, and a silver watch that my father sent me through the lines. Please take them off when I am dead, and give them to Captain Irvine, to give to my father when he gets back home. Here are my clothing and blanket that anyone who wishes them may have. My rations I do not wish at all. My gun and cartridge-box I expect to die with."

In a skirmish, two days later, Bob and Sam survived through the heaviest firing of the day. As Sam pointed out to Bob that the expected death had not occurred, a solid shot struck Bob at the hip, tearing off a leg and scattering his intestines. He shrieked,

> "Oh, oh God"

and expired immediately.

PRESTON SMITH

Brigadier General CSA

Chickamauga, Georgia, September 19, 1863

Trying to co-ordinate an attack after sundown, Smith discovered that soldiers advancing in the center had moved off line and had then halted, blocking the troops moving up on the flank. Riding forward to reorganize his men, Smith, in the dark, rode up to the Federal lines and, not realizing these were not his troops, demanded to know who was in command. Although some reports indicate that he and his aide were killed instantly by Federal troops, one report claims that before he died he said simply,

> "It was my duty." *

WILLIAM HAYNES LYTLE

Brigadier General USA

Chickamauga, Georgia, September 20, 1863

Surrounded by Confederates, he ordered a charge. Leading his troops he said,

"If I must die, I will die as a gentleman. All right, men, we can die but once. This is the time and place. Let us charge."

During the advance, he was hit in the spine, then by three more bullets. He murmured,

"Brave, brave, brave boys—"

before drowning in his own blood.

CHICKAMAUGA SOLDIER

USA

Chickamauga, Georgia, September 20, 1863

After the battle he lay on the field beyond help, his bowels protruding. In agony he cried,

"Jesus, have mercy on my soul!"

"REBEL COLONEL"

CSA

Chickamauga, Georgia, September 20, 1863

Seeing twelve-year old Johnny Clem, the Colonel reined up his horse and demanded,

"Stop, you little Yankee devil!"

Clem swiftly raised his rifle and shot the Colonel off his horse.

DUNCAN J. HALL

Lieutenant Colonel USA

Chickamauga, Georgia, September 20, 1863

Shot through the bowels by a musket ball while he was leading the 89th Illinois Infantry, Hall told fellow officers,

"Tell my parents I died for my flag and my country. Tell my regiment to stand by their flag and country."

Later, left on the battlefield, Hall was approached by a Confederate officer who offered aid. Hall made a request:

"I am dying. Wash me clean and bury me decently."

In answer to the Confederate's question, Hall identified himself as

"Lieutenant Colonel D. J. Hall of Chicago."

The Confederate then administered some morphine and Hall died soon after. The Confederate marked the grave with a crude headboard.

BATTLE OF THE WILDERNESS

MICAH JENKINS

Brigadier-General CSA

The Wilderness, Virginia, May 6, 1864

On the second day of fighting, as the Confederate generals under General James Longstreet reorganized in order to resume battle, twenty-nine year old Jenkins from South Carolina rode cheerfully to the front despite the illness from which he was still recuperating. Bolstered by Longstreet's successful flank attack, but aware of the difficulties ahead, Jenkins, shaking hands with his friend Colonel Ashbury Coward, said,

"Old Man, we are in for it today."

Attempting to inspire the men of the 6th South Carolina, Jenkins rode in front of them and shouted,

"Now, boys, don't get scared before you get hurt."

His confidence high, Jenkins organized a cheer for General Longstreet. Then he joined General Joseph Kershaw at the head of the column. Riding near General Longstreet, Jenkins offered congratulations to his superior and stated confidently,

> "I am happy; I have felt despair of the cause for some months, but am relieved, and feel assured that we will put the enemy back across the Rapidan before night."

Just then Confederate troops, in confusion, fired on their own men. Longstreet was wounded; two officers killed. Jenkins was shot in the head, the damage exposing part of his brain. Taken to the rear, he died near sunset without regaining consciousness.

MARCUS BAUM

Orderly CSA

The Wilderness, Virginia, May 6, 1864

Hastily galloping into camp, Baum spoke with a doctor to whom he uttered his last recorded words:

> "I must go to him [General Kershaw] at once. The General sent me off with a message."

Hastily he dashed off, and after successfully maneuvering through deadly fire, joined the head of Kershaw's column, only to die in the same volley that killed Brigadier General Micah Jenkins.

SECOND VERMONT VOLUNTEER

USA

The Wilderness, Virginia, May 6, 1864

During an aggressive attack by the Confederates, this soldier, less intimidated than his fellows who were hugging the ground to avoid the minie balls, raised himself up in order to re-load more quickly. Shot in the chest, he stumbled backward, exclaimed,

"I am killed!"

and fell on top of a companion.

THOMAS J. MOUNGER

Private, CSA

The Wilderness, Virginia, May 6, 1864

As the Confederates reached the Federal breastworks, Thomas Mounger of the 9th Georgia Infantry was hit by a minie ball that severed his jugular vein. Perhaps realizing that the wound was fatal, he turned to a lieutenant and asked,

"Where is John?"

His brother, John Mounger, had been killed in the same attack just minutes earlier. Sitting down behind the breastworks, Thomas quickly bled to death.

HARMON ROBINSON

CSA

The Wilderness, Virginia, May 10(?), 1864

Wounded and captured, Robinson of the 8th Georgia lay in the Union field hospital, compassionately aided by one James E. Smith who took the time to write a letter for Robinson to his sisters.

> "Dear Sisters:
>
> While lying here under the shade of these pines, I am having this man write a few lines to you to let you know that on last Friday I had the great misfortune to get a very severe wound in the battle of that day by a minie ball. It passed through my left hip very high up and smashed it very badly, and it is so high up that the doctor says he can't do anything for me. After I was shot, I was taken by the enemy and am now at their hospital among their wounded and some few of ours are here. The surgeon told me today that there was no hopes of my living. But while there is life, there is still hopes."

BATTLE OF SPOTSYLVANIA

National Archives
The Last Words of General John Sedgwick were repeated wherever old soldiers gathered.

JOHN SEDGWICK

General, USA

Spotsylvania, Virginia, May 9, 1864

Unable to advance because of Confederate sharpshooters, the Union artillery was forced to keep its distance. As sharpshooter bullets kept the artillerists under cover, Sedgwick tried to motivate his men by standing and shouting encouragement.

> "What! What! Men dodging this way for single bullets! What will you do when they open fire along the whole line? I am ashamed of you. They couldn't hit an elephant at this distance."

When another soldier, reacting to the shrill sound of a passing bullet, dove for the ground, Sedgwick nudged the man with his foot and said,

> "Why, my man, I am ashamed of you, dodging that way. They couldn't hit an elephant at this distance."

When the soldier arose and said that he believed in dodging, Sedgwick laughingly said,

> "All right, my man; go to your place."

As Sedgwick spoke with an officer, another shrill whistle was abruptly ended with the unmistakable sound of a bullet hitting flesh. Sedgwick, blood spurting from a hole under his left eye, fell heavily to the ground.

J. R. MONTGOMERY

Courier, CSA

Spotsylvania, Virginia, May 10, 1864

Mortally wounded in the first defense of the Bloody Angle, Montgomery of the 11th Mississippi used his last hours to write a letter to his father, the paper stained by his blood.

Spotsylvania County Va
May 10 1864

Dear Father

This is my last letter to you. I went into battle this evening as courier from Genl Heth. I have been struck by a piece of shell and my right shoulder is horribly mangled & I know death is inevitable. I am very weak but I write to you because I know you would be delighted to read a word from your dying son. I know death is near, that I will die far from home and friends of my early youth, but I have friends here too who are kind to me. My Friend Fairfax will write you at my request and give you the particulars of my ~~requests~~ death. My grave will be marked so that you may visit it if you desire to do so, but is optionary with you whether you let my remains rest here or in Miss. I would like to rest in the grave yard with my dear mother and brothers but its a matter of minor importance. Let us all try to reunite in heaven. I pray my God to forgive my sins & I feel that his promises are true(?) that he will forgive me and save me. Give my love to all my friends. My strength fails me. My horse and equipments will be left for you. Again a long fairewell to you. May we meet in heaven.

Your Dying son,
J. R. Montgomery

JAMES CLAY RICE

General, USA

Spotsylvania, Virginia, May 10, 1864

Brought to the rear with a shattered limb, Rice underwent surgery but realized he was dying. He said,

"Turn me over."

To the surgeon's query as to which direction, Rice, who could clearly hear the sounds of battle, replied,

"Let me die with my face to the enemy!"

MAINE SOLDIER

USA

Spotsylvania, Virginia, May 10, 1864

Wounded in the chest by large canister shot in a late afternoon charge, he lay on the battlefield near the Confederate lines. When Confederate soldiers began roaming the field, he caught the attention of Major Stiles and asked him,

"Can you pray, sir? Can you pray?"

With Stiles' prompting, the soldier repeated a simple prayer until death took him:

"God have mercy on me, a sinner, for Jesus Christ's sake."

CHARLES L. COLEMAN

Lieutenant, CSA

Spotsylvania, Virginia, May 12, 1864

Having removed their artillery in preparation for Grant's retreat, the Confederates were taken by surprise when Grant chose to attack at the Mule Shoe defenses. By the time the guns could be replaced, the Federal soldiers were overwhelming the Confederate position. As one panicking soldier asked for directions for pointing the gun, Coleman, wounded, had only breath enough, before dying, to say,

"At the Yankees."

ABNER MONROE PERRIN

Brigadier General, CSA

Spotsylvania, Virginia, May 12, 1864

In search of glory, Perrin joined the desperate defense of the Mule Shoe. As he rode toward the fighting he proclaimed:

"I shall come out of this fight a live major general or a dead brigadier."

He was shot from his horse as he led his men into battle.

HOSPITAL DEATHS 1863~1865

BUD CRAIGHEAD

Private CSA

Near Perryville, Kentucky, January, 1863

Seriously wounded in the leg, he was bed-ridden for three months. His family, having first heard that he had been killed, was overjoyed to journey to his bedside and remain with him until he recovered. In January his condition deteriorated and he believed he was dying.

> "God Bless you all! Then Ma won't have her son...I'll be in heaven. I'll watch over you all when I go there. God bless. God bless you...Don't cry for me!"

He lingered in agony for a few more days.

> "Sis, for heaven's sake give me something...Pa, please throw me out the window or break my poor leg off—anything to ease me."

EDWARD HOSMER

Sergeant, USA

Baton Rouge, Louisiana, January 24, 1863

Gradually wearing away, pale and wasted, twenty-year old Edward lay in hospital for days, suffering with fever. On the morning of his demise, he greeted his older brother James who cared for him daily and who often remained with him at night:

> "I am glad to see you again."

When James refused an impracticable request, Edward said,

> "Oh, never mind. Just as you say."

After a sip of brandy, he died swiftly and quietly.

ELIJAH S. BROWN

Private USA

Hammond Hospital, Point Lookout, February 4, 1863

Elijah Brown of the 2nd Vermont Regiment died of disease on February 4, 1863. His last letter, written for him by a friend, was addressed to his sister.

> "Hammond Hospital Jan 23rd 63
> Dear Sister
> It has been a pretty long time since I have written to you but you must not think I have forgotten you. One reason I have to offer is, and I think is a pretty good one, I have been very sick and am pretty sick yet but hope in a few days to be better. I received a

letter from father this morning and he says he is enjoying good health. The Vermont commissioners have been round to Washington and vicinity taking the troops home. I wish they would come around here and visit some of us because this is an exceedingly dull place for a sick man. I see cousin Moses Leech the day I left Fairfax Seminary Hospital. He came as far as the boat with me. He was well and hearty. I don't know of any news to tell you of so I will close by sending my respects to all, asking you to please write soon and often to your absent, but affectionate, brother,

E. S. Brown."

DISCHARGED INVALID

USA

Chicago, Illinois, Spring 1863

Just four hours from his home in Wisconsin, the dying soldier, accompanied by nurse Mary Livermore, missed the Saturday train and was forced to spend the night in Chicago. As nurse Livermore was leaving the hotel room to telegraph the soldier's mother, he said to her,

"I hate to have you go, for it seems as if I should not see you again."

When she returned an hour or so later, the man had died.

ROBINSON

Private USA

Near Philadelphia, Pennsylvania, April, 1863

Wounded almost a year earlier at the battle of Fair Oaks, Robinson was kept in hospitals, the wound refusing to heal. Though apparently becoming healthier, good-natured Robinson suffered a relapse eventually dying in a hospital bed, deliriously mumbling,

"I am out on the water, out on the water!"

THEODORE CHAPIN

USA

Nashville, Tennessee, June, 1863

Wounded at the Battle of Murfreesboro, he lingered in hospital for six months before succumbing to his wounds. In January, believing he was dying, he wrote this letter to his wife:

"My Dearest, Dearest wife, my sweet, sweet babes, I am going to write a few lines to you ere my spirit takes its final leave. Last night the vital just flickered in its socket. Today I have a little added and will improve it in this way. It is hard for one to give it up for the sake of wife and babes and I have thought that I should not. I NEVER, NEVER should have been here....

In regards to paying the debts Sarah, I think it best to not pay the mortgage until the other debts are paid. If the Doctor should take advantage of it....

Now Sarah, my gentle patient wife, your Father, your Mother, your Edward, your Jacky, and my Sweet Babes, goodbye, goodbye. I have no doubt that letter [sic] shall reach you, and in all probability in less than 36 hours, my body will be in the ground and my spirit shall be with you if possible when you read this letter. They have removed me to another hos'l that makes no difference as I need not tell you where to direct any more. I have looked at your and Gene's likeness 26 times today and wished that I could be with them when I died."

WILLIAM P. YEARGIN

Private CSA

Chester, Pennsylvania, August 11, 1863

Captured at Gettysburg on July 2nd, Yeargan of Co. E, the 22nd Georgian Infantry, after having his left leg amputated, was brought to the U. S. A. General Hospital. The day before he died, the young Georgian fully understood when he was told that he should write to his family.

"You mean, then, that I must die?"

Asked if he were ready to die, he responded,

"Oh no! I am not prepared to go. My mother taught me, long years ago, my duty to God; she died praying for me, but I have forgotten it all, and now I am to die and be shut forever from her presence."

He then dictated messages home, ending,

"Father, brother, sisters, I hope to meet you in heaven."

The next day, as he weakened in bed, he requested,

"Turn me over, please, and put me on my knees."

Kneeling in the attitude of prayer, he died.

JIM'S FRIEND

USA

Washington, D. C., September 10, 1863

At Lincoln General Hospital, suffering from a wound in the left lung, this soldier became attached to a recuperating soldier, Jim Morrison of the 149th New York State Volunteers. Allowing only Jim to aid him, he returned Jim's kindness by presenting his silver hunter cased watch to Jim. Shortly before he died, in response to Jim's question as to whether he had any friends, he said,

"One. You."

SAMUEL BROWN COYNER

Captain CSA

Orange Court House, Virginia, September 16, 1863

Wounded while leading his men in a cavalry skirmish near Culpepper Court House on September 13th, he was taken to a hotel and tended by a doctor and, for an hour or so before he died, his sister. Following the doctor's advice not to let Coyner fall asleep, the sister asked if he recognized her. He said,

> "Oh, yes, my dear sister. Your face is always familiar, always before me."

And did he recognize the doctor?

> "Oh, yes, yes. Always the dear fellow."

As he failed rapidly, she asked again if he knew who he was. With his last breath, he said,

> "Your brother."

CHARLEY REASON

Private, United States Colored Troops

Beaufort, South Carolina, September (?), 1863

Wounded when the 54th Massachusetts Regiment, the first regiment composed of Blacks, charged Fort Wagner, Reason was taken to the new hospital for colored soldiers. Because of gangrene, Reason had to suffer a further amputation. The twenty-year old died with Dr. Esther Hawks by his side.

> "O yes! I know what I am fighting for. Only a few years ago I ran away from a man in Maryland who said he owned me and since then I've worked on a farm in Syracuse but as soon as the government would take me I came to fight, not for my country—I never had any—but to gain one. My mother died years ago...My mother was all I had to love me, and she has gone home, sweet home. I shall see her soon—I'm glad to go home. Pray with me...."

JOHN M. SPRINGER

Chaplain USA

Resaca, Georgia, May 15(?), 1864

One of many chaplains who suffered to minister to the soldiers, Springer succumbed to disease with his faith intact. His last words were,

> "It is all well."

STEWART C. GLOVER

Private USA

Washington, D. C., May 21, 1864

Wounded in the leg at the Wilderness, Glover of the 5th Wisconsin, was transported to a hospital in Washington after the leg was amputated. The twenty-year old suffered for sixteen days in the hospital where he kept a diary. On the day he died he wrote,

> "Today the doctor says I must die—all is over with me—ah, so young to die."

On another page, he left a note to his brother:

> "Dear brother Thomas, I have been brave but wicked—pray for me."

CHARLES CUTTER

Private USA

Washington, D. C., May 22, 1864

Brought to the hospital with a mortal wound in his abdomen, seventeen-year old Cutter of the 1st Massachusetts Heavy artillery lay quietly in the heat, fanned by hospital volunteer, poet Walt Whitman. As Cutter opened his eyes, he heard Whitman ask if something was wrong. Cutter merely smiled and said,

> "Oh, nothing. I was only looking around to see who was with me."

Young Cutter drifted in and out of consciousness and died during the night.

NED WILLIS

Colonel CSA

Chickahominy River, Virginia, May 30, 1864

Mortally wounded, Willis lay in the field hospital attended by a doctor and a friend, Sandy Pendleton. When Sandy arrived, Willis said,

> "Sandy, the doctors won't tell me whether I am going to die. Am I mortally wounded?"

When Sandy replied in the affirmative, Willis continued,

"That's right, old fellow; that's the way I like to hear a man talk. I am not afraid to die any more than I was afraid to go into battle."

After Sandy hoped that Willis had good cause not to fear death, Willis responded:

"I trust so, Sandy. I believe I have."

After the doctor's protest that there was a small chance of recovery, Willis stated:

"I am very glad there is a chance to get well, but I am not afraid to die. Doctor, if I die, will it be today and will I suffer much pain?"

The doctor confirmed that death would be soon, but painless. Then, asked by Sandy if Willis wanted to see anyone else, Willis said,

"Yes, Moxley Sorrel's sister to whom I am betrothed. I am not afraid to die. I don't mind it myself, but it will almost break her heart and my poor Father's and Mother's. Tell her not to be distressed. I die in the best cause a man could fall in."

He died about an hour later.

LYMAN A. ROGERS

Captain USA

Washington, D. C., July 10, 1864

Wounded in the left leg at Cold Harbor on June 2 while leading a charge, Lyman of the 98th New York Volunteers suffered an amputation before being brought to Armory Square Hospital in Washington. Recuperating nicely, on June 26th he wrote a letter to his father:

"I trust that the prayers that have been offered up for me have been heard. I try to pray myself. My ideas upon the subject of religion have changed a good deal. I hope that in the event of my getting well, and mingling in the gay scenes of the world, these thoughts may not be dissipated, and I become as thoughtless as before. I hope you will continue to pray for me, that if in God's mercy I am to be restored to health I may be soon with you again; but if in the dispensation of Providence I am not to recover, pray that I may join the sainted ones gone before."

When complications arose, he reacted to the doctor's news that he did not have many hours to live:

"If I die I die of an honorable wound. I die for my country."

He died peacefully.

NATHAN NEWTON

Private CSA

Only fifteen years old, Nathan suffered for six weeks before dying in delirium. The boy-soldier died calling,

"Mother, mother. Mother, come here."

MARGARET E. BRECKINRIDGE

Nurse USA

Niagara Falls, New York, July, 1864

After nursing soldiers in a Baltimore hospital, Breckinridge over-exerted herself helping soldiers on a hospital steamer on the Mississippi River. Unable to fully regain her health, she continued to work toward returning to the war hospitals to, as she wrote the Hospital Commission,

> "do a little to atone for the great evils which some of [my] kinsmen had inflicted upon [my] beloved country."

After helping to return the body of her soldier brother-in-law to Niagara Falls, she fell ill and died five weeks later, whispering to a deathbed friend,

"Underneath are the everlasting arms."

WILLIAM BEAVENS

Lieutenant CSA

Winchester, Virginia, July 31, 1864

Wounded in the leg on July 18th, twenty-four year old Beavens had the leg amputated on the 19th and he was then removed to York Hospital in Winchester. There he grew attached to his nurse Kate Shepherd. Contracting typhoid fever, Beavens grew weaker and, when Miss Kate said she would be away for a day, he said,

> "I'll not see you again. I am almost gone. I am not afraid to die."

As Kate encouraged him with words and jelly, he admitted,

> "I would like to get well for the sake of my parents. I would love to see them—but I will not on earth."

Knowing Miss Kate had to leave, he said,

> "Thank you, thank you for all you have done for me."

Later he became delirious, dying about five o'clock on that hot afternoon.

HENRY C. CARPENTER

Corporal CSA

Woodstock, Virginia, October 6, 1864

Carpenter of the 45th Virginia Infantry dutifully wrote his sister reporting on the daily events of a soldier's life. He died of disease in the camp hospital, unafraid and

"willing to die." *

In his last moments he was delirious, calling out to his brother who was in a prisoner of war camp:

"Eddy, Eddy, Eddy." *

"OLD GRAY-HAIRED SIRE"

Private CSA

Montgomery, Alabama, October 17, 1864

Dying in Concert Hall Hospital, the elderly soldier, ready to go "home" at last, told his ward mates:

"I have not heard from home in a long time, but I may meet some of my people in the other world when I get there, and I shall go in a few hours."

HENRY H. GRANGER

Lieutenant USA

City Point, Virginia, October 30, 1864

Wounded on October 27th at Hatcher's Creek after positioning his six three-inch guns, Granger of the 10th Massachusetts Light Artillery was taken to a hospital. On the day he died he told a friend to pass on a message to his soldier uncle:

"Tell Uncle I am not afraid to die. I was ready to obey my last order."

JOHN HOWARD KITCHING

Colonel USA

Dobb's Ferry, New York, January 10, 1865

Wounded at Cedar Creek three months earlier, the twenty-six year old Kitching did not live to enjoy his promotion to Brevet Brigadier General. Before the operation, which he did not survive, he said to his sister,

"It will all be over in a few minutes, darling, and we will have such a nice talk afterward."

JAMES McCHESNEY

Private USA

Washington, D. C., May 28, 1865

Wounded at Petersburg with the 147th New York Infantry on March 30, 1865, twenty-year old McChesney was taken to Campbell Hospital. Because his wound was in the spine, doctors could do little for him and his condition deteriorated. Like many debilitated patients, he used the services of a selfless letter writer to communicate with his parents.

"Campbell Hospital
May 21st 1865

My health is not as good as when I wrote before. I have been confined entirely to my bed and have bed sores more painful than my wound which I believe is getting along as well as could be expected. My wound affects spine; therefore have no power over my lower limbs.

I am in a deplorable condition. To live I never would be any comfort to my self nor to my friends and the doctor says that I cannot live many days. I am failing fast. I have to be turned every five minutes. They have a comfortable bed as can be fixed. I am now on a water bed which is very comfortable. They take as good care of me as you could if you had me at home so you need not worry about me for they are doing everything that can be done for anybody.

You need not build yourself up with the hope of ever seeing me alive because I may not live....

... I send my undying love to you all and still hope to see you all on earth."

Written for James Mchesney [sic] by a friend in the Hospital.

Most respectfully Oliver C. Clark.

Library of Congress

Hospital tents behind Douglas Hospital, Washington.

ANDERSONVILLE

Andersonville became the most notorious of the Civil War prisons. Because of a lack of resources and General Grant's policy of not exchanging prisoners, Andersonville soon became overcrowded. In the last year of the war, Federal prisoners suffered severely from unsanitary conditions and inadequate food and shelter. Nearly 13,000 prisoners died in the camp.

PATRICK DELANY
Private, USA
Andersonville, Georgia, July 11, 1864

While in prison, Delany and others formed a gang of "raiders" to intimidate and rob, often with violence, other prisoners. Finally confronted and restrained by a group of prisoner "regulators", the prison authorities allowed the prisoners themselves to try the raiders; Delany and five others were sentenced to hang. With materials provided by the authorities, the regulators built a scaffold. Moments before he fell through the trap, Delany said,

"Boys, God be with you all, and me."

ALFRED H. VOORHEES
USA
Andersonville, Georgia, August 13, 1864

During his three-month incarceration in Andersonville Prison, Voorhees of the 1st New York Cavalry kept a diary. On July 28th, he wrote:

> "Very unhealthy in this place, quite a number die daily. I don't feel well, have the Diarhea very bad. More Yanks came in to day, had quite a heavy shower."

On the 29th, he continued:

> "Hot and dry till night When we had a small Shower. More Yanks came in today 700 from every army. am quite bad to day hop[e] to be better soon, it is very disagreeable to be sick in this place. George is very bad. Talk of a Parole the 6th of August, hope it will be so for I want to go home out of this Bull Pen."

On August 3rd, he made his last entry:

> "Hot and dry, am very stiff in My neck and arms, so I can scarcely get them to my head. Tis very disagreeable to be in this Bull Pen. Took quite a number out to day."

Too ill to continue with the diary, he was one of those "taken out" to the Andersonville cemetery ten days later.

FREDERIC AUGUSTUS JAMES

Landsman USN

Andersonville, Georgia, September 15, 1864

Serving aboard the U. S. S. *Housatonic,* James was captured in an attack against Fort Sumter after he and others had made a landing. The heavy fire forced the ships to retreat. He was eventually taken to Andersonville prisoner of war camp where he kept a diary, making his last entry when his health began to deteriorate.

> "Saturday Aug. 27th.
>
> Sunday 21st Misty & showery with some sun now & then. Eat a bisquit, a boiled egg & a small yellow tomato (@.10) & some tea for supper. Monday 22nd Cloudy in the forenoon but we had some sun in the P. M. Did not wash out my underclothes as I did not feel as well as I have averaged lately. Eat some raw potato as I begin to suspect that the scurvey is at the bottom my troubles. Tuesday 23rd Pleasant. Wore a wet girdle last night & had a cloth on my head & so slept more comfortably than I have done for some nights past."

Despite his concern about scurvy, he died of dysentery and chronic diarrhea.

SAMUEL MELVIN

Private USA

Andersonville, Georgia, September 25, 1864

Weakened by scurvy, Melvin of the 1st Massachusetts Heavy Artillery, was completely exhausted after helping with the wreckage of a derailed train some miles from the prison. Taken to hospital, he recorded his last words in his diary on September 15th.

"I want to go home."

MAY 1864~AUGUST 1864

JAMES EWELL BROWN (JEB) STUART

Major General CSA

Richmond, Virginia, May 12, 1864

As General Stuart attempted to retake his defenses at Yellow Tavern, one of the retreating Federal soldiers, possibly John A. Huff, fired a desperate shot at an imposing Confederate officer. Unknowingly, Huff had wounded Jeb Stuart, famous for his brilliant raids in Federal territory.

Stuart was carried behind the lines and endured a painful trip to Richmond. In a relative's home, aware that he was dying, he made his final arrangements. At one point he said,

> "I am resigned if it be God's will, but I would like to see my wife."

Along with two ministers he sang "Rock of Ages" and, shortly thereafter, he died. His wife did not arrive in time.

THOMAS A. McLEAN

Lieutenant CSA

Resaca, Georgia, May 14, 1864

While in the trenches under heavy artillery fire, McLean was hit with a shell that tore his leg off. Two other men were killed by the same shell. As men scrambled to leave the trench that had become a deathtrap, McLean, despite his wound, tried to control them.

> "Be steady, men; don't let them see any confusion. They will know they have our range and make it worse for us."

A second shell landed near McLean, killing him and a stretcher-bearer.

GEORGE A. TAYLOR

Captain USA

Rome Cross Roads, Georgia, May 16, 1864

Taylor of the 66th Illinois, perhaps misunderstanding his orders to secure a road or perhaps seeking greater glory, continued his advance beyond the road. While steadying his men, he was killed by a bullet in the head. Before going into battle, he had said,

> "I will either have a larger stripe on my shoulders or I will leave my body on the field."

WILLIAM LYMAN

Private USA

Fredericksburg, Virginia, May 20, 1864

Lyman of Company M, First Massachusetts Heavy Artillery, lingered one day after being wounded. Six days earlier he had written a final letter to his wife:

> "I feel rather sad when thinking of dear ones at home and the uncertainty of ever seeing them again. But think not that I am afraid to do my duty. If my health is spared me, you will not hear that I have shrunk from duty, however arduous and perilous it may be; and if it should be my fortune to fall at my post, tell our dear children that their father died to transmit to them, untarnished, the best Government that the world ever knew. Tell them, if they live to be men, to go and do likewise, if occasion should require it."

TROOP H CAVALRYMAN

USA

Haw's Shop, Virginia, May 23, 1864

In one of the most fierce cavalry encounters of the war, the dismounted trooper, shot in the breast, stumbled toward Major Kidd, falling into his arms and uttering,

"Oh, Major!"

SOUTH CAROLINA SOLDIER

CSA

Haw's Shop, Virginia, May 23, 1864

As the Union cavalry overwhelmed the Confederates, this soldier, whose surrender was demanded by Union cavalryman Sergeant Avery, went down fighting after saying,

"I have no orders to surrender, damn you!"

JAMES CUMMINGS

Sergeant USA

Dallas, Georgia, May 25, 1864

Even though no battle seemed imminent, Cummings of the 123rd New York Volunteer Infantry told a friend that he had a presentiment of his own death, perhaps even that day. Several hours later the regiment was hurried forward as reinforcements. As dusk approached, the fighting subsided into skirmishing, most of the men lying down on the rain-soaked ground. Six-foot, four-inch Cummings arose and stood leaning on his musket despite the warning of his friend. Calmly he said,

"I don't think there is any more danger in standing here than lying in the mud. I have had enough of that."

Less than a minute later, he tumbled to the earth, shot in the forehead. Taken to the field hospital, he died before morning.

STEPHEN ALBERT ROLLINS

Color-Sergeant USA

Cahawba, Alabama, June 16, 1864

Mortally wounded at the "Guntown fight" near Guntown, Mississippi on June 10th, Rollins of Company B, 95th Illinois Infantry, was captured and taken to the Confederate prison at Cahawba. Shortly before he died, he said,

"My faith in my country has ever been firm!"

"FRED"

CSA

Cold Harbor, Virginia, June, 1864

As the soldiers huddled in the trenches in the days following the Cold Harbor battle, three brothers were visited by their younger brother, Fred, on his way home because of wounds received at the Wilderness. After waiting for soldiers to write hasty letters for him to carry home, Fred rose up on his crutches and said,

"Well, let me take a good look at those rascals over the way, for it will be a long time before I get another chance."

He tumbled back into his brothers' arms, another victim of a sharpshooter.

BLACK SOLDIER

Private

55th Massachusetts Regiment USA

James Island, South Carolina, July 2, 1864

He and many of his black comrades went into battle remembering the black soldiers who surrendered at Fort Pillow, Tennessee in April, only to be mercilessly shot by the Confederate soldiers who often viewed black soldiers as runaway slaves. Many of his regiment, the 55th Massachusetts, died shouting,

"Remember Fort Pillow!"

WILLIAM A. GRAHAM

Sergeant(?) CSA

New Hope Church, Georgia, July 4, 1864

At dawn on Independence Day, as Graham, enjoying an early morning pipe, was standing near the protective works, a sharpshooter's bullet struck him in the chest. As men picked him up to carry him to the rear, he said,

> "Boys, it is useless. Please lay me down and let me die."

He accepted death philosophically, dying in a few minutes.

GRIFFIN A. STEDMAN, JR.

Colonel USA

Near Petersburg, Virginia, August 6, 1864

Anticipating an attack in the late afternoon of August 5th, Colonel Stedman, though warned not to expose himself, surveyed the trenches and terrain and determined that the slackening of the Confederate firing indicated that no attack was imminent. While he and General Ames were discussing the situation in the trench, everyone in the vicinity heard the unmistakable sound of a bullet hitting flesh. As General Ames inquired as to who was struck, Stedman reached into his coat, brought out a blood-stained handkerchief and said,

> "I believe I am hit."

Though attempting to walk away, he lost strength and lay down, saying,

> "General Ames, I don't believe I shall recover from this."

Taken to his tent at headquarters, Stedman received medical aid, mainly a little morphine. Around eight o'clock he asked the doctor,

> "How long is it likely that I shall live?"

At this moment, a friend entered and Stedman, cool and calm, said,

> "Well, Davis."

In halting sentences he explained:

> "I was too confident, Davis, too confident. I did not think that I should be struck. I have escaped so many times and when the danger was so much greater. It seems too bad to be shot in this insignificant skirmish."

Unable to continue he merely said,

> "It gives me great pain to talk."

Though his friend tried to comfort him, Stedman faced his reality:

> "So my career is ended."

As his pain increased, he begged the doctor,

"Oh! Put me to sleep now!"

When the morphine proved inadequate and his suffering grew, he urged yet again,

"Oh, Doctor, put me to sleep; put me to sleep quickly!"

Several administrations of chloroform were required to settle him. As he drifted off, he mumbled brokenly, only once speaking clearly as if giving an order:

"Let there be no delay."

Then he slept, dying about 7:30 in the morning.

FEDERAL SCOUT

USA

Near Romney, West Virginia, August 6(?), 1864

One of two "Jessie Scouts" disguised in Confederate gray riding some distance ahead of the rest of the company, he and his partner surprised Confederate officer H. Gilmor who quickly shot and killed the second scout. At the mercy of Gilmor, the quick thinking Scout cried out,

"What the hell are you doing? You are killing your own men!"

In reply to Gilmor's question as to which command the Scout belonged, he responded,

"To Captain Harry Gilmor's command."

Though shrewd, he was not quick enough to realize that Gilmor had been promoted to major a year earlier. Gilmor killed him.

NOLAN

Captain, USA

Reams Station, Virginia, August 25, 1864

After an aborted charge, Captain Nolan of Company B ordered his men back to reform. As the Confederates advanced, Nolan moved down the line encouraging the men to stand their ground and hold their fire. Shot in the chest, he fell, giving his last order with his dying breath:

"Tell Captain Taggart, Company I, to take command."

BATTLE OF ATLANTA

JAMES GALBREATH

Private CSA

Near Atlanta, Georgia, July 22, 1864

Nearing Atlanta, Galbreath took every opportunity to kneel and pray.

> "O, my poor wife and children! God have mercy on my poor wife and children! God pity me and have mercy on my soul!"

Reprimanded for demoralizing the other soldiers, he refrained from kneeling but continued to mutter to himself. As the battle started, a cannon ball caught Galbreath and he died muttering,

> "O, God have mercy on my poor soul."

National Archives

James McPherson rode into battle but did not watch his back.

JAMES BIRDSEYE McPHERSON

General USA

Near Atlanta, Georgia, July 22, 1864

As McPherson's soldiers moved toward Atlanta, McPherson learned that his left was in danger of attack. Riding toward the action with his orderly, he received a bullet in the back and fell from his horse. When the orderly asked him if he were hurt, he replied,

> "Oh, orderly, I am."

His body quivered and in moments he was dead.

THOMAS JEFFERSON ENNIS

Major USA

Ezra Church, Georgia, July 28, 1864

Leading his regiment in a move to counteract a right flank sweep, Ennis was mortally wounded with a bullet in the intestines. Two agonizing hours after the injury, he was visited by his friend General John Corse. Ennis said,

"Is that you, General?"

In response to Corse's offer of aid, Ennis replied,

"General, I cling to life with the tenacity of a drowning man to a straw, but I know there is no hope for me. Telegraph my brother."

After a pause, his features brightened,

"Did we whip them?"

Assured that they had whipped them, he whispered,

"Thank God."

CULPEPPER

CSA

Near Atlanta, Georgia, July 31, 1864

Having worked up a thirst digging ditches, Culpepper and a companion took their canteens and walked to the well. A sharpshooter's bullet struck Culpepper in the head. He lived for ten hours, sometimes calling out the name of a friend:

"Bill. Water."

TURNER

Private USA

Near Atlanta, Georgia, August, 1864

While waiting for his meal, cup and plate in hand, young Turner had the misfortune to be hit in the left shoulder by a stray bullet. As he was put on a stretcher, he asked,

"Boys, what's the matter? What makes it so hard for me to breathe?"

Moments later he was dead.

WILLIAM B. BROWN

Major USA

Near Atlanta, Georgia, August 3, 1864

Leading the men of the 70th Ohio in an attack to take the enemy's skirmish pits, he was hit in the side by a minie ball. Before losing consciousness, he said,

"Boys, take the works, and tell the general I died at my post, doing my duty."

His soldiers successfully completed their task.

BATTLE OF NEW MARKET

WILLIAM SPALDING

Captain, USA

New Market, Virginia, May 15, 1864

As he led Companies A and B of the 18th Connecticut into New Market Valley, Spalding encountered heavy resistance from Major General Franz Sigel's forces. Despite repeated warnings from his men, he refused to take cover and was shot in the stomach. Taken to the rear, he lingered for an hour, his last question to the surgeon indicating his concern over the outcome of the fight.

"Are they driving us?"

JOHN A. CHRISTMAN

Private, USA

New Market, Virginia, May 15, 1864

As the 12th West Virginia was moved into the line, Christman received a bullet in the heart, the only man in his outfit to be killed. Moments before he was hit, he tempted fate by jokingly stating,

"I hope I will be killed today."

TWO ANONYMOUS PRIVATES

CSA

New Market, Virginia, May 15, 1864

Lying wounded with a third companion after fierce fighting with the 18th Connecticut, the two privates of the 51st Virginia shouted encouragement to the passing Cadets who were moving up to the front lines.

Private #1:

"Charge them, boys! Charge them!"

Private #2:

"Give the yankees hell!"

As the wounded soldiers waved their hats, a shell landed among them, killing all three men.

WILL DAY

Sergeant CSA

New Market, Virginia, May 15, 1864

As Company A of the Missouri Cavalry attacked the enemy's cannons, Day, shot in the chest, staggered toward his commander, First Lieutenant Edward H. Scott, took Scott's hand and died immediately after saying

"Lieutenant, I am almost gone. Please help me off."

NEW MARKET SOLDIER

Private, CSA

New Market, Virginia, May 15, 1864

Immediately after the death of Will Day, this Private of Company A, Missouri Cavalry, his jugular severed and pouring blood, saw Lieutenant Scott nearby and called out,

"Goodbye, Lieutenant. I am killed."

WILLIAM B. BACON

Captain USA

New Market, Virginia, May 15, 1864

Captain of the 34th Massachusetts, he was mortally wounded and borne from the field. With the idealism of youth, not yet twenty-one years old, he uttered:

"Tell them I died fighting for my country."

Virginia Military Institute

Cadet Thomas G. Jefferson was one of 258 cadets who stepped forward to fight for the exhausted South.

THOMAS GARLAND JEFFERSON

Cadet, CSA

New Market, Virginia, May 18, 1864

Major-General Breckinridge was forced to order cadets into battle when a large gap appeared between his forces. Four cadets were killed almost immediately, six died later. Jefferson fell, wounded in the stomach. After the battle he was taken to a home where, his mind wandering, he died two days later. Just before dying, he said to a friend,

"Duncan, come and light a candle. It is growing dark."

BATTLE OF COLD HARBOR

CAMPBELL

Gunner CSA

Cold Harbor, Virginia, June 2, 1864

The day before the major battle while the armies maneuvered men and supplies, Gunner Campbell provided covering fire with his artillery piece and repeatedly ignored those who cautioned him about standing erect. Finally hit by a minie ball, he shouted,

> "Oh, God! I'm done forever!"

Lying near the gun, he watched others continue the assault until his replacement suggested they cease fire. With his last breath, Campbell replied,

> "Well, if you think it's safe, Adjutant! Tell my mother I died like a soldier."

COLD HARBOR DIARIST

USA

Cold Harbor, Virginia, June 3, 1864

After a terrible assault, a young Federal soldier lay on the battlefield, wounded and dying. Because a cease-fire to remove the dead and wounded could not be arranged, he and many others had time to reflect on their desperate situations. In his blood-stained diary he made his final entry:

> "June 3. Cold Harbor. I was killed today."

AUGUSTUS W. GRAY

Sergeant CSA

Division Hospital, Gaines' farm, Virginia, June 3, 1864

Wounded on June 1st by a minie ball that broke his spine, the Georgia soldier lingered for two days. On the night after he was wounded, he gave his visiting comrades this advice:

> "Boys, prepare for death. Read the scriptures and pray often. Prepare to meet your God."

In the hours before his death, he told his brother,

> "Jim, I cannot be with you long. I know I must die. I want you to write to Mary and tell her not to grieve after me. Tell her to raise the children the best she can. Instruct them and raise them so that they would know good from evil."

Near death, he said to his brother,

> "Tell Mary and my children to meet me in Heaven."

PETER A. PORTER

Colonel USA

Cold Harbor, Virginia, June 3, 1864

Expecting to charge at dawn, Porter of the 8th New York Heavy Artillery remained alert all night. As the men formed their ranks, a soldier suggested the charge might be "foolish" and that many men might not survive. Porter firmly said,

> "That has nothing to do with the matter. If I am ordered to cross there, I shall go, and I think my regiment will follow me."

Leading his men in the charge, Porter was hit in the chest. Falling to his knees, he shouted,

> "Close on the colors, boys!"

Another enemy volley cut him down.

SCOTT

CSA

Cold Harbor, Virginia, June 4?, 1864

After the battle, as Scott and other former Yale men reminisced in the trench about Old Yale, someone asked Scott if it was his turn to fill the canteens at the spring. Scott said,

> "Yes, I believe it is. Pass up your canteens."

In an exposed stretch, Scott met death from the rifles of several Federal sharpshooters.

COLD HARBOR SOLDIER

USA

Cold Harbor, Virginia, June 5, 1864

Attempting to force General Grant to admit defeat, General Lee would not allow the removal of the wounded from the battlefield unless Grant asked for a truce. Unwilling to admit defeat, Grant waited four days before finally conceding to a truce. By then, this Cold Harbor Soldier, like most of the wounded, had died after suffering in the heat, begging,

> "Water, water, for God's sake, water!"

ALLEN MOORE

Gunner CSA

Cold Harbor, Virginia, June 5?, 1864

As evening approached, Gunner Moore, despite sharpshooters, insisted on sighting his artillery piece. Warned by his captain not to expose himself, Moore persisted:

> "One moment, Captain! My trail's a hair's breadth too much to the right!"

A moment later, a bullet smashed into Moore's head.

BATTLE OF KENNESAW MOUNTAIN

SAMUEL BEARD

Private USA

Kennesaw Mountain, Georgia, June 18, 1864

With only 400 yards separating the two forces, Co. D prepared for sleep. Beard spread out his blanket and, still standing, stretched his arms upward. At that moment he was hit by a random shot. In bewilderment, he looked toward his friend and, before taking his last two steps, said,

> "Oh, Frank, I am killed. They have shot me through the lungs."

THOMAS P. WIMMS

Private CSA

Kennesaw Mountain, Georgia, June 20, 1864

Under constant fire, Wimms and others began to tire and grow careless. As evening approached, Wimms climbed out of the trench and lay down. Warned by an officer that he was dangerously exposed, Wimms replied:

> "I am sleepy for I was out there on picket all last night and I am going to have a good stretched out sleep if they kill me for it."

Ten minutes later, the officer found him dead, shot in the body.

GREEN H. LASSITER

Private CSA

Kennesaw Mountain, Georgia, June 20, 1864

While sleeping in the trench, Lassiter awoke to a terrible pain. A bullet had struck him in the abdomen and tore its way into his chest. In great agony he prayed:

> "Blessed Virgin! Have mercy on me!"

Death came within fifteen minutes.

TONGUELESS SOLDIER

USA

Kennesaw Mountain, Georgia, June 27, 1864

Shot in the mouth, a minie ball tearing out his tongue, the young soldier staggered to a friend and made motions indicating paper and pencil. Supported by his friend, the dying man wrote on the blood-stained paper:

> "Father, meet me in Heaven."

Before he could sign his name, he expired.

BATTLE OF PETERSBURG

EDWARD M. SCHNEIDER

Private USA

Petersburg, Virginia, June 19, 1864

The seventeen-year old former student of Phillips Academy lay mortally wounded after a charge by the 57th Massachusetts. To the attending chaplain he said,

> "I have a good many friends, schoolmates, and companions. They will want to know where I am,--how I am getting on. You can let them know that I am gone, and that I die content. And, chaplain, the boys in the regiment,--I want you to tell them to stand by the dear old flag! And there is my brother in the navy,--write to him and tell him to stand by the flag and cling to the cross of Christ!"

After being told by the surgeon that he would die soon, Schneider replied,

> "Yes, doctor, I am going home. I am not afraid to die. I don't know how the valley will be when I get to it, but it is all bright now."

He then sang, probably with the chaplain, a verse often sung by the soldiers:

> "Soon with angels I'll be marching,
> With bright laurels on my brow;
> I have for my country fallen,--
> Who will care for sister now?"

Though in pain, he suffered quietly until death came.

FREDERICK PETTIT

Corporal, USA

Petersburg, Virginia, July 9, 1864

A veteran of several battles, Pettit had been wounded and, upon rejoining his regiment just two days earlier, had discovered that he had been promoted. The closeness of the two armies created many opportunities for sharpshooters on both sides. Pettit, not accustomed to this sniper warfare, continued his habit of writing almost daily to his family. His last letter was written about six o'clock in the evening, only an hour or so before a sharpshooter's bullet struck him in the neck while he sat reading:

"Dear sister Mary:

I received your very kind letter of the 4th inst. Today. I was very glad to get it indeed. It is only the second letter I have received since I was wounded. I wrote a letter home on Sunday from Camp Distribution.

The same night about 10 o'clock we left that place and went on board the steamer Spaulding at Alexandria bound for City Point. We remained at anchor in the river until about 8 o'clock on the morning of the fourth when we started down the river. The day was very fine and if we had been less crowded would have had a very pleasant time. A few miles below Alexandria we passed Mt. Vernon, the home of Washington, a spot dear to every loyal heart. The grounds and buildings are almost entirely concealed by the thick groves of shade trees which surround them. This is almost the only point of interest in passing up and down the Potomac.

About midnight we passed Fort Monroe and at 11 o'clock on the 5th we came in sight of City Point. This is quite a business place now, the wharf being crowded with steamers, schooners, and barges discharging their cargoes of commissary, quartermaster, and ordinance stores. The railroad is now in running order about 6 miles from the landing.

We went on shore about noon (there was about a thousand of us) and in the afternoon we started for the front. It was quite warm and the dust was almost intolerable. We camped for the night about 21/2 miles from the front. The next day we went on to Army Headquarters on the extreme left of the line and then back about 5 miles to the regiment where I arrived about 1 o'clock.

I found them in the front line about 2 miles from Petersburg and about 500 yds. from a rebel fort. The pickets keep up an incessant firing along the line night and day which is relieved every 5 minutes by the mortars and siege guns throwing shell back and forth.

Our division is now divided into two brigades and we hold a line the length of a brigade, there being two lines of works. Each brigade remains in the front line 3 days and is then relieved by the other brigade. There is not much advantage in being in the rear line as both lines are equally exposed to the enemy's fire and it is necessary to keep under cover.

The boys here in front are much more cheerful and confident than in the rear about Washington and Philadelphia. The men are well satisfied with the campaign thus far and put great confidence in the government and General Grant. My health is good and I am getting along finely. D. Wilson is now in the hospital sick. I have not seen him but understand he had been sent to City Point. J. R. Evans, Pence, and the rest are well.

Write again soon. Send me some papers and whatever reading matter you can. We get very lonesome lying in the ditches with nothing to do but watch the rebels.

The 76th P. V. are lying near us. I went to see them on Thursday. D. Shoemaker, D. Allen, and J. C. Grandy are with the regiment and are well. They say they never saw anything like this before. I saw C. M. McCoy at Philadelphia. He is slightly wounded in the arm. Andrew Lary is now guarding cattle. I have not seen him since I came back.

I think that if Nye and Kelty try their missionary scheme on the old plan they may expect some success. There is indeed a wide field of Christian usefulness in that section. But Nye's ambition to establish a new society in that place will never succeed. Any established society in the neighborhood might find it a profitable field for missionary effort.

But I must close. The day is warm and cloudy and the usual amount of firing is going on. There has been no rain here for two months.

When I returned to the regiment I was quite surprised to find my name at the end of the list of corporals of Co. C. It was a thing I did not expect. I shall try to do my duty.

Write soon and send along those papers, magazines, or whatever you can find in the reading line.

Your brother,
Fred Pettit
Co. C. 100th P.V.

ANONYMOUS BLACK SOLDIERS

USA

Petersburg, Virginia, July 30, 1864

Attempting to end the siege of Petersburg, General Grant's men tunneled under the Confederate artillery bastion, loaded the cavity with gunpowder and blew up the guns along with 278 Confederate soldiers. As part of the attack, Ferrero's black soldiers skirted the enormous crater, singing as they blundered into a Confederate counter-attack.

> "We looks like men a-marching on;
> We looks like men of war."

A third of the division was killed or wounded.

THOMAS H. ROCKWOOD

Major US Colored Troops

Petersburg, Virginia, July 30, 1864

Rockwood led colored troops into the battle of the Crater. As he and his troops reached the crest of the Crater, he shouted,

> "Hurrah!"

but was instantly killed.

FORMER BARBER

Private US Colored Troops

Petersburg, Virginia, July 30, 1864

After the battle, lying mortally wounded near the edge of the Crater, he recognized a Confederate soldier, Colonel Frank Huger, whom he used to shave before the war. Despite being on opposite sides, the dying black man reached out to Huger's humanity, saying,

> "Mass Frank, please, Mass Frank, can I have some old greasy water what they been washing dishes in? I don't want no good water but just old greasy water they are going to throw away."

The gift of a little water was all that could be done for him.

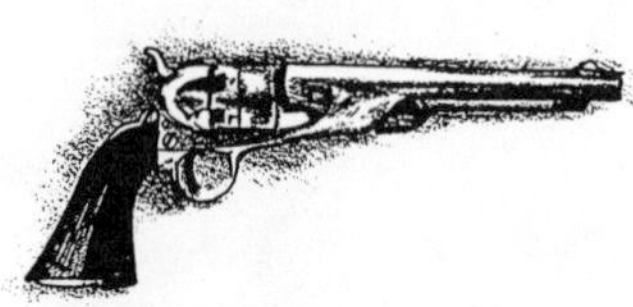

BATTLE OF JONESBORO

NEW YORK YANKEE

Jonesboro, Georgia, September 1, 1864

As the Confederates desperately built breastworks in an attempt to delay the Federal army's advance, a New York regiment charged. Nearing the defenses, "one great big Yank" leaped up on the breastworks and demanded:

"Surrender, you damn rebels!"

He was immediately shot down.

HENRY C. BOYD

Lieutenant CSA

Jonesboro, Georgia, September 1, 1864

Promised reinforcements, the Confederates tried to hold their defenses despite the loss of their Battery. As the Federals continued their assault, many of them lying just on the other side of the breastworks, Lieutenant Boyd shouted,

"Never give up, boys!"

Boyd was immediately killed by a Federal soldier who was quick enough to leap to his feet and fire, but who was not quick enough to avoid a bullet in the head.

JOSEPH H. BENNER

Sergeant USA

Jonesboro, Georgia, September 1, 1864

One of several color bearers killed that day, Benner of the 74th Indiana was shot while he was in advance of the lines shouting,

"Boys, follow me!"

WILLIAM SHARP

Private, USA

Jonesboro, Georgia, September 1, 1864

The last of four brothers killed in the war, eighteen-year old Sharp, mortally wounded, called for his boyhood friend who was also in the 100th Indiana Infantry Volunteers. To his friend who had been his Sunday School companion, Sharp whispered,

"I wish I had been a better boy. I have not been as good as I ought to have been." *

With no one else willing to pray with Sharp, his boyhood friend knelt beside him and prayed until Sharp's spirit slipped away.

BATTLE OF CEDAR CREEK

DANIEL DAVIDSON BIDWELL

Brigadier General USA

Cedar Creek, Virginia, October 19, 1864

After Federal troops were surprised and routed by an early morning Confederate attack in the fog, Bidwell led a counter-attack that was quickly repulsed. During the attack he was hit by a shell fragment. At the field hospital, he said to the surgeon,

"Doctor, I suppose there is no hope of recovery."

Told that the wound was fatal, Bidwell said,

> "Oh, my poor wife. Doctor, see that my record is right at home. Tell them I died at my post doing my duty."

RODGERS

Sergeant CSA

Cedar Creek, Virginia, October 19, 1864

Wounded in the left breast, Rodgers, lying on the battlefield, spoke to a Federal soldier who was willing to take a message for family or friends.

> "If ever the war is over, and you can, write my father who lives in Quitman, Georgia, and tell him where I died."

After he supplied his father's address and name, William H. Rodgers, he was left to die on the field.

"HUSKY-VOICED SOLDIER"

Private, USA

Cedar Creek, Virginia, October 19, 1864

After the battle was over, this soldier lying on the field, his blue pants soaked with his blood, stopped his victorious General and other officers by calling,

"Hurrah for General Emory!"

When the General inquired about the seriousness of his wound, the man answered,

> "My leg is broken by a rifle shot. I suppose I shall lose it. But I still feel able to say, 'Hurrah for General Emory.' I fought under you, General, at Sabine Cross Roads and Pleasant Hill."

Though he was optimistic about recovering, his wound was high up on his thigh. His short gasps indicated he had little time left.

SEPTEMBER 1864~MARCH 1865

RUFUS RICKSECKER
First Lieutenant USA
Winchester, Virginia, September 19, 1864
On the day before the battle, he wrote his last letter home:

"Hd. Qrs. Co. "G" 126th O. V. I.
Sept. 18th 1864

My Dear Folks at Home,

I will this morning write a few lines before the trains go back to the Ferry.

I was very much surprised & shocked on opening your letter to hear of the sudden death of our dear Ma. I was not at all prepared for such a change in the family circle; I had just received the letter of Father the day before, & although he spoke of the severity of the disease, still it hardly seemed possible that the next mail would again leave me a motherless boy. Poor Charlie, what a blow to him it must be.

I suppose he could not get home to see her; I will try and write to him oftener as he will need all the sympathy we can give him. I was very, very glad to learn that you my dear Sister, had the helping heart and hands of dear Lottie, to minister to the wants of ma.

I hope and pray that the probable sickness of Father which Addie spoke of, has not been verified, & that he may be spared to us all for a long time.

How do you (Addie) intend to manage housekeeping? If Auntie could only be with you; but she needs rest herself & is getting old. Is Lottie still with you?

It is useless for me to offer any more of my poor expressions of feeling so we will drop the very painful subject hoping that we may really realize that "it is all for the best."

I am in very good health. We yesterday moved camp about 300 yards in order to get more room, as the Regiment has increased very much within the last 3 weeks. We now have a very fine camp & will have it in very good order if we do not have to leave this place; which by the way, we are at present very much afraid of as it is said Lt. Gen. Grant has come up to visit this department. We are ready to go but would much rather stay. I don't think there are many who would like to be started towards Petersburg. The Rebel statements that they have been whipping the 6th A. C. every few days are altogether untrue as we have not had even a skirmish with them since we have been at this camp. They pitch on the 8th & 19th A. C. once in a while, but they have been very careful to stay away from us, so far at least.

Well I hear the wagons rattling so I must close in a hurry. Hoping you are all well & will write as often as you can to

Your Son & Brother
Rufus"

While leading an attack the next day, he received three wounds, two of which, in the neck and abdomen, were fatal. As the company fell back, several comrades wished to carry Rufus but he said,

"It's no use, boys; I'm going to die. Save yourselves."

His friends removed his personal belongings, covered him with a blanket and left him to die.

PETER VREDENBURGH, JR.

Major USA

Winchester, Virginia, September 19, 1864

As Vrendenburgh led the 14th New Jersey Volunteers in a charge, he said,

"Guide on me, boys! I will do the best I can!"

He was instantly killed early in the charge when he was struck by a shell.

CAPTAIN

Louisiana Guard Artillery, CSA

Near Winchester, Virginia, September 19, 1864

As he rode between the guns cheering on his gunners, the Captain was hit by a shell that tore away his arm. Turning in the saddle so that his men would not see his wound, he shouted,

"Keep it up, boys! I'll be back in a moment!"

Attempting to ride to the rear, he died in the saddle and fell.

W. H. LATHROP

Colonel USA

Sulphur Branch, Tennessee, September 25, 1864

After Confederates took the fort at Athens, they moved toward a string of defensive blockhouses. At the badly constructed and incomplete blockhouse protecting Sulphur Branch trestle bridge, Lathrop determined to make a desperate stand. Dying from the blast of the second Confederate shot, Lathrop futilely urged his men,

"Do not surrender the fort."

Heavily outnumbered, the next commanding officer surrendered and the bridge was destroyed.

ALBERT V. E. JOHNSTON

Major USA

Near Centralia, Missouri, September 27, 1864

Arriving in Centralia with the 39th Missouri Infantry, Johnston was informed that guerillas under Bloody Bill Anderson had stopped a train earlier that day and killed over twenty unarmed Union soldiers who were passengers. Johnston and his men approached the guerilla camp about two miles from Centralia. The guerillas, warned by their scouts, had formed a battle line but did not immediately attack. Johnson ordered a dismount, prepared his men, all new recruits, and shouted a challenge to the guerillas,

"We are ready! Come on!"

When no attack was forthcoming, he shouted again,

"Wait for us, you damned cowards!"

The guerillas mounted and charged. Though Johnston ordered the use of bayonets, his men broke, almost all of them being killed. Johnston died in a revolver duel with guerilla Jesse James.

"REBEL CAPTAIN"

CSA

Richmond, Virginia, October, 1864

Leading his men forward, the Rebel Captain, when only fifteen yards from the line of Federal soldiers who held their fire, planted his regiment's flag and shouted,

"Now, you damned Yankees, there is our flag! We will fight for it!"

He died in the first volley, a ball entering his eye.

HENRY WARD CAMP

Major USA

Near Richmond, Virginia, October 13, 1864

Leading a charge through a thicket of scrub oaks, Camp of the 10th Connecticut Infantry urged on his men by shouting,

"Come on, boys! Come on!"

Despite a withering fire from the flanks, Camp advanced to within a few yards of the enemy lines before he was shot down and his men retreated.

AARON WOLFORD

Private USA

Griswoldville, Georgia, November 22, 1864

Patriotic forty-four year old Wolford, father of eight, was called "Uncle Aaron" by the younger men of the 100th Indiana Infantry Volunteers with whom he often prayed when the chaplain was absent. The night before he died he replied to his eighteen-year old picket duty companion who wanted to know what was troubling him:

> "I do not know, but I feel that I have not long to live and when I am gone I want you to promise me that you will take charge of my things. Send them to my wife and write to her all about me."

The next day, in battle, he died instantly, shot in the head.

ROBERT GOODING

Lieutenant USA

Nashville, Tennessee, December 16, 1864

While waiting for the attack in which he died, Gooding had his attention drawn to a house that was similar to one owned by Gooding's brother Charles.

> "Yes. Something tells me I'll never see Charles' house again."

A bullet through the heart proved him true.

JAMES HOOVER

Private USA

Near Stevenson, Alabama, January 31, 1865

As the soldiers were being transported from Huntsville, Alabama to Nashville, Tennessee, Hoover, slightly drunk, fell between two boxcars as the train was in motion but he managed to grab on to the coupling. His call for help brought a cook to his rescue but the man could not pull Hoover aboard. As Hoover's legs banged against the rails, both Hoover and the cook lost strength. Hoover begged,

"Let me go! My legs are broken!" *

The cook finally had to release his hold and Hoover fell beneath the wheels.

WILLIAM (?) B. (?) CHERRY

Sergeant USA

Near Columbia, South Carolina, February 15, 1865

Though the anxiety of waiting for a fight often made him physically ill, Cherry of Company K, 100th Indiana, invariably performed bravely once the fighting began. While waiting to cross a stream, Cherry's colonel scolded him for being ill, and shamed him into going to the front. Cherry retorted,

"I will go, Colonel, since you insist, but I am sure if I go up there I shall be killed."

Ten minutes later he was instantly killed by the last shot from the Confederate battery.

JOHN I. WORTHINGTON

Major USA

King's River, Arkansas, March 13, 1865

During a charge at King's River, eighteen miles from Fayetteville, Worthington of the 1st Arkansas Cavalry was shot in the breast. Seeing the enemy routed, he urged,

"Go on, boys, and whip them! They have killed me."

He died fifteen minutes later.

CALVIN F. HARLOWE

Sergeant USA

Fort Stedman, Virginia , March 25, 1865

During a surprise night attack, Harlowe, a veteran of four years, and others of the 29th Massachusetts Regiment were quickly taken by Confederate soldiers who demanded his surrender. Although resistance was useless, with the words,

"Never while I live!"

Harlowe fired at the Confederate captain who shot at Harlowe simultaneously. Both men were killed.

BATTLE OF SAYLER'S CREEK

STAPLETON CRUTCHFIELD

CSA Colonel

Sayler's Creek, Virginia, April 6, 1865

While reporting to the generals, the dour artilleryman was hit by a shell that passed through both legs as well as the horse he was riding. He died within minutes. To those attending him, he said,

"Take my watch and letters for my wife. Tell her how I died, at the front."

STANDARD BEARER'S BROTHER

Lieutenant CSA

Sayler's Creek, Virginia, April 6, 1865

Although surrounded and outnumbered, the Confederate soldiers charged and a standard bearer was killed while speaking to his commanding officer, Major Stiles. As Stiles stooped to pick up the flag, a Lieutenant, brother to the fallen standard bearer, stepped over his brother's body and grasped the staff.

"Those colors belong to me, Major!"

Claiming the flag, he fell backward, shot through the head.

COLOR GUARD

Lieutenant CSA

Sayler's Creek, Virginia, April 6, 1865

Immediately after the death of the standard bearer and his brother, another Lieutenant, a member of the color guard reached for the flag, saying,

"Give them to me, Major!"

but he was killed before he could place his hand on it.

CHARLES W. GLEASON

Captain USA

Sayler's Creek, Virginia, April 6, 1865

Knowing that the end of the war was near, Gleason, who had risen through the ranks, asked,

"Colonel, are we to fight again?"

When the Colonel made an affirmation, Gleason cheerily said,

"Well, this will be the last battle if we win, and then you and I can go home. God bless you, Colonel."

Just as the battle started, Gleason was shot in the head.

JAMES DEARING

General CSA

Sayler's Creek, Virginia, April 6, 1865

Leading a charge to protect a bridge, Dearing's troopers were surprised by a cavalry attack. In a saber duel with the Federal Commander, General Theodore Read, Dearing mortally wounded Read but was in turn shot by Read's orderly. Later, visited on his deathbed in a nearby farmhouse by General Thomas Rosser and Colonel Elijah White, the man who had successfully completed Dearing's cavalry attack, Dearing pointed to his new brigadier stars and, nodding in the direction of White, said to Rosser,

"These belong on his collar."

GROANING SOLDIER

CSA

Sayler's Creek, Virginia, April 6, 1865

As the Confederates retreated, this private, shot through the legs and his body, was left lying in the leaves, groaning. He was found by a Union soldier who offered help.

> "Thank you for your sympathy, but no one can help
> me now. It will not be long till death relieves me."

Then, as the Union soldier started to leave, he had a second thought:

> "Yes, Yank, there is something you might do for me.
> You might pray for me before you go."

After a brief prayer, he was left on the field to die.

APPOMATTOX

WILLIAM PEGRAM

Colonel CSA

Five Forks, Virginia, April 1, 1865

The handsome young artillery officer rode to his battery as the Federals attacked. He gave his last order:

"Fire your canister low, men!"

Then he fell from his saddle into the arms of W. Gordon McCabe. Knowing that he was of no more use on the battlefield, he said,

"Oh, Gordon, I'm mortally wounded. Take me off."

Outflanked, the battery was quickly overrun.

5th CORPS PRIVATE

USA

Five Forks, Virginia, April 1, 1865

As the skirmish line faltered, General Philip Sheridan encouraged the men. One private near Sheridan fell to his knees, blood spurting from a wound in his throat. He shouted,

"I'm killed!"

Prompted by Sheridan's comment that he wasn't really hurt, the private rejoined the charge only to fall dead after a few steps.

RELUCTANT PRISONER

Private CSA

Five Forks, Virginia, April 1, 1865

Taken by surprise, he and a large number of soldiers quickly surrendered only to discover that the prisoners outnumbered their Union captors. Realizing he might still have a chance, he shouted,

"We can whip you yet!"

Grabbing a musket, he shot a captain and was then bayoneted as all the men resumed fighting.

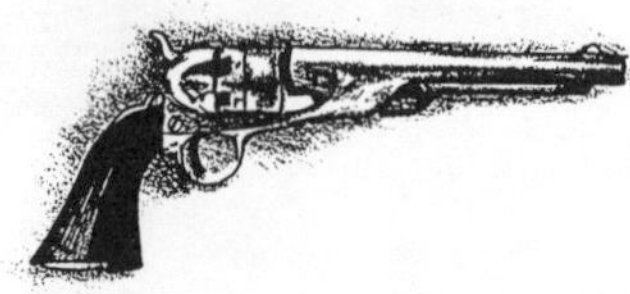

MORRISON

Private USA

Five Forks, Virginia, April 1, 1865

After the capture of a large body of Confederate soldiers, Morrison, an exceptionally strong man, and three others made their way through the prisoners. Leading the way, Morrison said,

"Come on, boys, and we will capture the flag!"

When the prisoners, discovering they outnumbered their captors, decided to continue the fight, Morrison and his three comrades were trapped, surrounded by the enemy. Though Morrison shouted,

"We will fight our way back to the regiment!"

two of the four men were killed, Morrison fighting fiercely to the end.

AMBROSE POWELL HILL

CSA General

Near Petersburg, Virginia, April 2, 1865

As soldiers skirmished in the mist, he rode up to two Federal privates and ordered:

"Surrender, or I'll shoot you! Troops are coming in from our left!"

The privates, who did not recognize him for a general, chose to shoot rather than surrender.

National Archives

Ambrose P. Hill could not convince two skirmishers to surrender.

SUICIDAL SOLDIER

USA

Near Petersburg, Virginia, April 2, 1865

After a failed charge, the private, left near the Confederate lines because his thigh was broken, saw Confederate soldiers running toward him.

"God damn you Johnnies! Get away from me! I'll not be taken!"

When the Confederates refused to put him out of his misery, the young man cut his own throat with a pocketknife.

REGRETFUL SOLDIER

CSA

Near Petersburg, Virginia, April 2, 1865

Away from the action, the regiment was surprised by shells unexpectedly coming from the Federal battery. The soldier, hoping for a chance to prove himself, was one of the first men mortally wounded.

"This is rough on me. If I had been killed in battle I wouldn't have cared, but to be shot in a skirmish it's too bad."

FORT GREGG DEFENDER

CSA

Fort Gregg, Virginia, April 2, 1865

Outnumbered ten to one, the defenders of Fort Gregg fought desperately, their efforts giving General Lee time to retreat and regroup before the Federal armies could trap him at Petersburg. As the first Federal soldiers breached the defenses at Fort Gregg, they ordered the doomed defenders to surrender. The heroic response,

"You'll see us in hell first!"

ignited fierce hand to hand combat in which 85% of the Confederates were casualties.

CONFEDERATE CAPTAIN

CSA

Fort Gregg, Virginia, April 2, 1865

As the Federal attackers swarmed over the heavily outnumbered Confederates, he roared above the din,

"Never surrender to the damned Yankees!"

Two Federal soldiers clubbed him to death with their muskets.

ARTILLERY OFFICER

CSA

Near Petersburg, Virginia, April 2, 1865

As General Lee's defense of Petersburg collapsed with the capture of his guns, an artillery officer, mortally wounded and propped up against a carriage shaft, answered two questions for a Union officer.

Whose battery?

> "Captain Williams' North Carolina, of Poague's Battalion."

Who was the officer on the gray horse?

> "General Robert E. Lee, sir, and he was the last man to leave these guns."

OSMOND B. TAYLOR

Captain, CSA

Amelia Court House, Virginia, April 6, 1865

As the Federal armies blocked the Confederate movements, Taylor's command was surprised by Custer's cavalry. Before being overwhelmed, Taylor's gunners managed a couple rounds of canister. Called on to surrender, Taylor was shot down just after giving his response:

> "I'll be damned if I do!"

National Archives

"The rest is silence."

LAST WORDS OF THE GENERALS

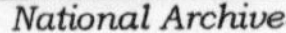

National Archives

Library of Congress

GRANT'S SURRENDER TERMS

Appomattox Court House, Virginia, April 9, 1865

"In accordance with the substance of my letter to you of the 8th instant, I propose to receive the surrender of the Army of Northern Virginia on the following terms, to wit:

"Rolls of all the officers and men to be made in duplicate, one copy to be given to an officer designated by me, the other to be retained by such officer or officers as you may designate; the officers to give their individual paroles not to take up arms against the Government of the United States until properly exchanged and each company or regimental commander to sign a like parole for the men of his command.

"The arms, artillery and public property are to be parked and stacked, and turned over to the officer appointed by me to receive them. This will not embrace the side-arms of the officers, nor their private horses or baggage. This done, officers and men will be allowed to return to their homes, not to be disturbed by United States authority so long as they observe their paroles and the laws in force where they may reside."

LEE'S ACCEPTANCE OF SURRENDER TERMS

Appomattox Court House, Virginia, April 9, 1865

Lieut. Gen. U. S. GRANT:

GENERAL: I have received your letter of this date containing the terms of surrender of the Army of Northern Virginia as proposed by you. As they are substantially the same as those expressed in your letter of the 8th instant, they are accepted. I will proceed to designate the proper officers to carry the stipulations into effect.

R. E. LEE
General

LEE'S LAST ORDER

GENERAL ORDER No. 9
Appomattox Court House, Virginia, April 10, 1865

After four years of arduous service, marked by unsurpassed courage and fortitude, the Army of Northern Virginia has been compelled to yield to overwhelming numbers and resources.

I need not tell the brave survivors of so many hard fought battles, who have remained steadfast to the last, that I have consented to this result from no distrust of them.

But feeling that valor and devotion could accomplish nothing that could compensate for the loss that must have attended the continuance of the contest, I determined to avoid the useless sacrifice of those whose past services have endeared them to their countrymen.

By the terms of the agreement officers and men can return to their homes and remain until exchanged. You will take with you the satisfaction that proceeds from the consciousness of duty faithfully performed, and I earnestly pray that a Merciful God will extend to you His blessing and protection.

With an unceasing admiration of your constancy and devotion to your country, and a grateful remembrance of your kind and generous consideration for myself, I bid you all an affectionate farewell.

LAST WORDS OF THE CONFEDERATE STATES OF AMERICA

With the fall of Richmond, the Government of the Confederate States fled to Danville, Virginia. As Lee made his final desperate maneuvers, President Davis optimistically issued an official proclamation to the southern people on April 4, 1865. As events moved quickly, it was to be his last proclamation:

> To the People of the Confederate States of America
>
> The General in Chief of our Army has found it necessary to make such movements of the troops as to uncover the capital and thus involve the withdrawal of the Government from the city of Richmond.
>
> It would be unwise, even were it possible, to conceal the great moral as well as material injury to our cause that must result from the occupation of Richmond by the enemy. It is equally unwise and unworthy of us, as patriots engaged in a most sacred cause, to allow our energies to falter, our spirits to grow faint, or our efforts to become relaxed under reverses, however calamitous. While it has been to us a source of national pride that for four years of unequaled warfare we have been able, in close proximity to the center of the enemy's power, to maintain the seat of our chosen Government free from the pollution of his presence; while the memories of the heroic dead who have freely given their lives to its defense must ever remain enshrined in our hearts; while the preservation of the capital, which is usually regarded as the evidence to mankind of separate national existence, was an object very dear to us, it is also true, and should not be forgotten, that the loss which we have suffered is not without compensation. For many months the largest and finest army of the Confederacy, under the command of a leader whose presence inspires equal confidence in the troops and the people, has been greatly trammeled by the necessity of keeping constant watch over the approaches to the capital, and has thus been forced to forgo more than one opportunity for promising enterprise. The hopes and confidence of the enemy have been constantly excited

by the belief that their possession of Richmond would be the signal for our submission to their rule, and relieve them from the burden of war, as their failing resources admonish them it must be abandoned if not speedily brought to a successful close. It is for us, my countrymen, to show by our bearing under reverses how wretched has been the self deception of those who have believed us less able to endure misfortune with fortitude than to encounter danger with courage. We have now entered upon a new phase of a struggle the memory of which is to endure for all ages and to shed an increasing luster upon our country.

Relieved from the necessity of guarding cities and particular points, important but not vital to our defense, with an army free to move from point to point and strike in Detail the detachments and garrisons of the enemy, operating on the interior of our own country, where supplies are more accessible, and where the foe will be far removed from his own base and cut off from all succor in case of reverse, nothing is now needed to render our triumph certain but the exhibition of our own unquenchable resolve. Let us but will it, and we are free; and who, in the light of the past, dare doubt your purpose in the future?

Animated by the confidence in your spirit and fortitude, which never yet has failed me, I announce to you, fellow-countrymen, that it is my purpose to maintain your cause with my whole heart and soul; that I will never consent to abandon to the enemy one foot of the soil of any one of the States of the Confederacy; that Virginia, noble State, whose ancient renown has been eclipsed by her still more glorious recent history, whose bosom has been bared to receive the main shock of this war, whose sons and daughters have exhibited heroism so sublime as to render her illustrious in all times to come—that Virginia, with the help of the people and by the blessing of Providence, shall be held and defended and no peace ever be made with the infamous invaders of her homes by the sacrifice of any of her rights or territory. If by stress of numbers we should ever be compelled to a temporary withdrawal from her limits, or those of any border State, again and again will we return, until the baffled and exhausted enemy shall abandon in despair his endless and impossible task of making slaves of a people resolved to be free.

Let us not then despond, my countrymen; but relying on the never-failing mercies and protecting care of our God, let us meet the foe with fresh defiance, with unconquered and unconquerable hearts.

JEFFERSON DAVIS

National Archives

In his last official proclamation, President Jefferson Davis, facing defeat, was still optimistic that the Confederacy could survive.

LAST WORDS OF A UNION SOLDIER

JENKIN LLOYD JONES

Madison, Wisconsin, July 18, 1865

Artilleryman Jones summed up the hopes and sentiments of thousands of men who returned quietly to civilian life. He lived a long and rewarding life, publishing his Diary in 1914.

> "Madison, Tuesday, July 18. The rolls have returned with Lieutenant Colonel Giddings' (mustering officer) signature annexed, and the military tie which bound us together as the 6th Battery has ceased to exist.
>
> 10 A. M. we assembled once more and in the yard in front of Captain Simpson's office, in the city of Madison, signed the final pay rolls, and received the much-coveted scrip "Discharge", bearing date of July 18. "Mustered out of United States service on the 3rd of July". It was not an hour of noisy demonstration, but happiness too sweet for utterance prevails, the emotion of thankfulness filling the dullest breast. "Free! Free!" was the exclamation of many as they became possessors of the prizes.
>
> But to me it brought many dark and serious thoughts to mind. Yes, free, but for the first time in my life I am my only dictator as to what course to pursue. Have arrived at age with life's issue fairly before me, and undecided what course to pursue. Inclination and duty seem strangely at variance. I must strive to attain the highest good that lies in my power. The dictates of conscience shall be my guide. To-night I retrace my steps to my quiet valley home. The many tender ties which bind me to my comrades of the march, battle and camp, are more than likely forever broken on this earth. And the diary which I have kept unbroken is hereby ended with the end of my service, having lived two years and eleven months in the service of my country. Three of the best years of my life have been lost to self-instruction, and the plans and hopes of my childhood have been ruthlessly toppled down, but the time has not been lost. I have no regrets for the way it has been spent. My prayer is that the remainder of my life may be as usefully spent. So, dear Diary, good-bye!
>
> Jenk. Ll. Jones"

LAST WORDS OF A CONFEDERATE SOLDIER

W. T. BUSSEY

Corporal, CSA

As the Confederate armies surrendered, each man was required to take an oath of allegiance to the United States, thus ending his participation in the Confederacy. After the oath was taken, the former soldier was free to return to his home.

"Headquarters U. S. Cavalry Corps

Griffin, Georgia: May1, 1865

> I, the undersigned W. T. Bussey, a Corporal of the Company "B", 9th Regiment of Georgia Military, do solemnly swear that I will not bear arms against the United States of America, or give any information, or do any military duty whatsoever, until regularly exchanged as a prisoner of war.
>
> [signed]
> W. T. Bussey"

END OF A CAREER AS A CIVIL WAR NURSE

A month or so after the war ended, as nurse Jane Stuart Woolsey drove away from the Washington hospital where she had cared for hundreds of soldiers, she had these thoughts, a poetic mixture of loss and joyless optimism.

> "In the still, fresh summer dawn we drove for the last time through the grove, down the long winding road to the highway leading to the City. The camp was silent and desolate, the store-room was empty and bare, the wards were quartermaster's lumber. Behind us the tower stood black against gray trailing clouds. Low flights of birds went circling round and round it. Before us the great dome showed spectral in the vapors of a sunrise that struggled and did not shine."

AFTERMATH

ABRAHAM LINCOLN

President of the United States
Washington, D.C., April 14, 1865

During the third act of *Our American Cousin* at Ford's Theater, Mary Lincoln took her husband's hand and wondered what their theater companion Miss Harris would think of Mary's "hanging on" to Lincoln. Lincoln replied,

"She won't think anything about it."

Moments later, John Wilkes Booth entered the Presidential Box and shot Lincoln in the back of the head. Without regaining consciousness, Lincoln died at 7:22 a.m. in the Peterson boarding house across the street from the theater.

National Archives

John Wilkes Booth fled Washington after assassinating Lincoln.

JOHN WILKES BOOTH

Actor
Near Port Royal, Virginia, April 26, 1865

After assassinating President Lincoln on April 14th, Booth escaped to Virginia where he was joined by fellow conspirator David Herold. While a fugitive Booth kept a diary in which he recorded his thoughts during his escape.

> "Until today nothing was ever thought of sacrificing to our country's wrongs. For six months we had worked to capture, but our cause being almost lost,

something decisive and great must be done. But its failure was owing to others, who did not strike for their country with a heart. I struck boldly, and not as the papers say. I walked with a firm step through a thousand of his friends, was stopped, but pushed on. A colonel was at his side. I shouted Sic semper before I fired. In jumping broke my leg. I passed all his pickets, rode sixty miles that night with the bone of my leg tearing the flesh at every jump. I can never repent it, though we hated to kill. Our country owed all her troubles to him, and God simply made me the instrument of his punishment. The country is not what it was. This forced Union is not what I have loved. I care not what becomes of me. I have no desire to outlive my country. The night before the deed I wrote a long article and left it for one of the editors of the *National Intelligencer,* in which I fully set forth our reasons for our proceedings. He or the gov'r-

After being hunted like a dog through the swamps and woods, and last night being chased by gunboats till I was forced to return, wet, cold and starving, with every man's hand against me, I am here in despair. And why? For doing what Brutus was honored for. What made Tell a hero? And yet I, for striking down a greater tyrant than they ever knew, am looked upon as a common cutthroat. My action was purer than either of theirs. One hoped to be great himself. The other had not only his country's but his own, wrongs to avenge. I hoped for no gain. I knew no private wrong. I struck for my country and that alone. A country that groaned beneath this tyranny, and prayed for this end, and yet now behold the cold hands they extend to me. God cannot pardon me if I have done wrong. Yet I cannot see my wrong, except in serving a degenerate people. The little, the very little, I left behind to clear my name, the Government will not allow to be printed. So ends all. For my country I have given up all that makes life sweet and holy, brought misery upon my family, and am sure there is no pardon in the Heaven for me, since man condemns me so. I have only heard of what has been done (except what I did myself), and it fills me with horror. God, try and forgive me, and bless my mother. Tonight I will once more try the river with the intent to cross. Though I have a greater desire

> and almost a mind to return to Washington, and in a measure clear my name—which I feel I can do. I do not repent the blow I struck. I may before my God, but not to man. I think I have done well. Though I am abandoned, with the curse of Cain upon me, when, if the world knew my heart, that one blow would have made me great, though I did desire no greatness. Tonight I try to escape these bloodhounds once more. Who, who can read his fate? God's will be done. I have too great a soul to die like a criminal. Oh, may He, may He spare me that, and let me die bravely. I bless the entire world. Have never hated or wronged anyone. This last was not a wrong, unless God deems it so, and it's with Him to damn or bless me. As for this brave boy with me, who often prays (yes, before and since) with a true and sincere heart—was it crime in him? If so, why can he pray the same?
>
> I do not wish to shed a drop of blood, but 'I must fight the course.' 'Tis all that's left to me."

Booth avoided the military pursuit with the aid of southern sympathizers until he and Herold were cornered in a barn. Herold surrendered but Booth called out,

> "Well, my brave boys, you can prepare a stretcher for me."

As the barn burned, Sergeant Boston Corbett spotted Booth in the barn and mortally wounded him. Booth was brought out to lie on the grass for two hours before dying.

> "Tell my mother...tell my mother that I died for my country."

Another source records a variation of his words as:

> "Tell my mother—I died—for my country....I thought I did for the best...."

Finally, looking at his hands, he muttered,

> "Useless! Useless!"

EDMUND RUFFIN

Southern Nationalist

Amelia County, Virginia, June 17, 1865

Though the south had surrendered, the seventy-two year old Ruffin, self-taught soil chemist, author and publisher, would not submit to Federal authority. On his last day (probably the 17th though he dated the entry as the 18th) before committing suicide at his plantation home of Marlbourne, the fiery secessionist, who has been credited with firing the first shot at Fort Sumter, wrote in his diary:

"I hereby declare my unmitigated hatred to Yankee rule—to all political, social and business connection with the Yankees and to the Yankee race. Would that I could impress these sentiments, in their full force, on every living Southerner and bequeath them to every one yet to be born! May such sentiments be held universally in the outraged and down-trodden South, though in silence and stillness, until the now far-distant day shall arrive for just retribution for Yankee usurpation, oppression and atrocious outrages, and for deliverance and vengeance for the now ruined, subjugated and enslaved Southern States!

Redmoor, June 18th 1865
Memoranda for the instruction of my son Edmund Ruffin jr.

As it is hereby avowed by me that my death will have been produced by my own will & act, there will be no necessity, or occasion, for the increased trouble & pain to the family in holding a Coroner's Inquest.

As my directions formerly given will not now be at hand, & may not be fully remembered, & would in part be now inapplicable, I will state here the most important & the changed circumstances.--I desire my death to cause as little trouble & difficulty as may be--& I earnestly request that my body may be buried within as few hours as will serve for the preparations to be indicated. Let my remains be buried in the clothes in which I shall die, & with merely the additional over-wrapping in an old sheet or blanket. The sooner a dead body is enveloped & in contact with the earth to which it is to return, & the more speedy its inevitable decomposition, & the disappearance of the corruptible portion, so much the better. I much prefer, & earnestly request, that there may be no coffin of any kind--& that I may be buried as usually were our brave soldiers who were slain in battle. Their manner of burial is quite good enough for me. But if this wish shall be deemed inadmissible, (as I fear it may be,) let the coffin be merely a rough oblong box, of the rudest materials & workmanship, without even being smoothed by the plane. Have no company assembled, other than the few nearest friends or neighbors, whose manual aid will be required for removing the body to the grave, (which shall be close at hand,) & covering it with earth. Do not have, or attempt to have, any religious or church or clerical ceremonies--which would now be improper, even if available & desired.

I request that none of my family or friends will wear mourning clothes for me--which custom is always useless & objectionable, & which, in. . . the condition of our country in latter years, & the recent & still continued destitution of the inhabitants, I deem to be inexcusably wasteful, & therein is even an offence against moral obligation. I ask the forgiveness of all my family & near friends to whom my latest act shall cause trouble or distress.

I give to my son Edmund the possession & charge (& property) of all my manuscripts. I earnestly request that none of them will be suffered to be lost by neglect, or destroyed by design, if possible to be avoided. I further desire that my own writings still unpublished, & of private character, (as are nearly all my manuscripts,) & all private letters directed to me, & both of dates since 1859, may be kept secreted from all unfriendly eyes, & only be permitted to be seen, if at all, by confidential friends, & at my son's will & discretion--so long as the people & the press of Virginia shall continue to be, as recently & now, enslaved & crushed by Yankee rulers & under an unrestricted despotism, aided by Virginia traitors & spies, both white & black.

I give my watch to my grandson George C. Ruffin.

And now, with my latest writing & utterance, & with what will be near to my latest breath, I here repeat, & would willingly proclaim, my unmitigated hatred to Yankee rule--to all political, social, & business connection with Yankees, & to the perfidious, malignant, & vile Yankee race.
Edmund Ruffin sen.

Kept waiting by successive visitors to my son, until their departure at 12:15 p.m."

Seating himself in a chair, he put a musket muzzle in his mouth and, using a forked hickory stick, forced the trigger. The cap exploded without firing the gun and the household was alerted. However, before anyone arrived, Ruffin replaced the cap and killed himself on the second attempt, the blast blowing off the upper portion of his head.

National Archives

Edmund Ruffin, credited with firing the first shot at Fort Sumter, committed suicide rather than live under Yankee rule.

National Archives

Mary Surratt required support on the gallows where she died with other Lincoln conspirators.

MRS. MARY EUGENIA SURRATT

Conspirator

The Old Penitentiary, Washington, D. C., July 7, 1865

A Confederate sympathizer and owner of the boarding house where the other conspirators met, forty-five year old Mrs. Surratt was implicated in the Lincoln murder and sentenced to hang. Soldiers supported her on the trip to the gallows where she sat on a chair until moments before the trap was released. She was helped to her feet and spoke:

"Please don't let me fall."

LEWIS THORNTON POWELL

Conspirator

Alias "LEWIS PAINE"

The Old Penitentiary, Washington, D. C., July 7, 1865

Having attacked Seward at Seward's home while Booth was killing Lincoln, Paine was convicted of conspiracy and went to the gallows with three other conspirators. As he stood on the gallows, he thanked the soldiers guarding him, then said,

> "Mrs. Surratt is innocent. She doesn't deserve to die with the rest of us."

Paine then co-operated with executioner Chris Rath who placed the noose around Paine's neck, verbally wishing Paine a quick death. Paine spoke cheerfully through the white hood:

> "You know best."

Library of Congress

Lewis Powell, conspirator in the Lincoln assassination, remained calm on the scaffold.

Library Of Congress

George Atzerodt lost his nerve before being hanged.

GEORGE A. ATZERODT

Conspirator

The Old Penitentiary, Washington, D. C., July 7, 1865

While his fellow conspirator, David Herold, remained silent but shaking, Atzerodt, a thirty-three year old German-born carriage painter, found his heavily accented voice just before the drop:

> "Good-bye, gentlemen. May we all meet in the other world."

HENRI WIRZ

Captain CSA

Washington, D.C., November 10, 1865

Wirz, the commandant of the infamous Andersonville Prison where Union prisoners of war were mistreated, was found guilty of murder. Shortly before being taken to the gallows, Wirz talked with Richard Winder. To him he said,

> "Dick, I am going, you know. These stories they have circulated about us are false. You will probably be made to suffer for a portion of these crimes they lay to me, but you are no more guilty than I, though just as much. Promise me, if you live, to do all in your power to wipe out this awful stain upon my character. Make my name and character stand as bright before the world as it did when you first knew me. Promise me you will do something to assist my wife."

The stoop-shouldered Swiss with "gray and restless eyes" drank whiskey before leaving his cell. On the gallows, amid hooting and jeering, Wirz heard the attendant soldiers chant, "Wirz, remember Andersonville." Major Russell shouted out the death warrant and then apologized to Wirz for having to carry out his unpleasant duty. Wirz responded,

> "I know what orders are, Major."

Then he spoke to the crowd:

> "And I am being hanged for obeying them."

A moment later he spoke to the priest who suggested a confession:

> "No, I am not guilty, Father."

Turning to the crowd he explained,

> "I go before my God—the Almighty God—who will judge between us. I am innocent and I will die like a man."

Another source reports he said:

> "This is too tight; loosen it a little. I am innocent. I will have to die sometime. I will die like a man. My hopes are in the future."

He then spoke to Captain Walbridge:

> "Goodbye, Captain. I thank you and the other officers of the prison, for you have all treated me well."

As the trap was sprung, the crowd cheered.

Library of Congress

Officials adjust the rope at the hanging of Confederate Captain Henri Wirz, commander of the notorious Andersonville Prisoner of War Camp.

ANTHONY P. DOSTIE

Dentist

New Orleans, Louisiana, July 30, 1866

An outspoken and intemperate leader for the enfranchisement of black men, Dostie, a white Radical, was instrumental in the movement to recall the Convention to rewrite the state constitution. In the Reconstruction era, he made several speeches that antagonized pro-slavery white men who were still a strong force in New Orleans. During the afternoon break in the Convention's meeting at the Mechanic's Institute, the delegates and a large crowd of black men were attacked by police, firemen and white citizens. In the riot, 37 people were killed, 146 wounded. Dostie, intending to surrender himself, implored the aggressors to spare his life. However, he was shot in the spine and stabbed with a sword in the stomach. Dragged through the gutters, he was eventually tossed on a trash heap. His last words are recorded as:

> "I am dying. I die for the cause of Liberty. Let the good work go on."

EXPLOSION OF STEAMBOAT SULTANA

In the early morning hours of April 27, 1865, the steamer *Sultana*, one of the largest sidewheelers on the Mississippi, churned up the mighty river a few miles above Memphis, Tennessee. With a legal capacity of 400 passengers, she was greatly over-loaded with approximately 100 civilians and crew and 2300 soldiers, most of them recently released from the southern prison camps at Andersonville and Cahaba and eager to return to their homes and families. At 2 a.m., as the *Sultana* neared a point called Paddy's Hen and Chickens, the boilers, repaired with a patch only a few days earlier at Vicksburg, exploded. The explosion and the resulting fire killed many of the passengers. Many more, still weak from their ordeal in the prison camps, died in the cold spring waters of the Mississippi River. That dark night, approximately 1800 people died, "crying, praying, screaming, begging, groaning and moaning." Aboard the burning boat could be heard "agonizing shrieks and groans." In the water, men could be heard singing or swearing, cursing incompetent leaders who had brought them to this tragic end.

GEORGE DOWNING

Private USA

Paddy's Hen and Chickens, Tennessee, April 27, 1865

Because he had been visiting friends in Memphis, Downing of the 9th Indiana Cavalry missed the departure of the *Sultana* from the Memphis dock. Feeling fortunate to have the money his family had sent to him at Vicksburg, he paid two dollars to be rowed out to the steamer that was across the river at the coaling station. Boarding the steamer, he expressed his relief to a friend,

> "If I had not sent home for that money I would have been left."

"VOLUNTARY MARTYR"

Civilian

Paddy's Hen and Chickens, Tennessee, April 27, 1865

As hundreds of men struggled in the water, some in their despair grasping others and dragging them under, a female member of the Christian Commission stood on the boat's deck and talked to the men in the water, "urging them to be men" and finally calming them. When the flames encroached, the men begged her to jump into the water but knowing that the men would attempt to save her perhaps at the cost of some lives, she refused to leave the deck. She explained,

> "I might lose my presence of mind and be the means of death of some of you."

Calmly she waited until the smoke and flames overcame her, one of twenty-two women who died in the tragedy.

KENTUCKY SOLDIER

USA

Paddy's Hen and Chickens, Tennessee, April 27, 1865

Pondering their dilemma, two Kentucky soldiers, aware that the riverbank was for them an impossible distance away, stood on the deck peering at the dark waters. Admitting to each other that neither one could swim, they recognized the reality of their situation. One said,

> "Then let us die together."

Holding to each other, they leaped to their deaths.

OLD SOLDIERS & OTHER NOTABLES

WINFIELD SCOTT

General USA

West Point, New York, May 29,1866

The old soldier played only a minor role near the beginning of the Civil War, giving up command of the army to younger men. He lived long enough to write his memoirs and see the south defeated. Near the end, his main concern was still that of a good soldier:

"Peter, take good care of my horse."

National Archives

Winfield Scott made a soldier's deathbed request.

ROBERT E. LEE

General CSA

Lexington, Virginia, October 11, 1870

Lee, tired when the war ended, struggled through the next five years, honored as the warrior who surrendered his army but not his dignity. In his final years he served as President of Washington College. Suffering a stroke at the end of September, 1870, he was bed-ridden, finally slipping into a coma on October 10th. His final words are recorded in a biography as the last wanderings of the old soldier:

"Tell Hill he must come up!"

and, a little later,

"Strike the tent."

However, biographer Emory Thomas claims that no such words were spoken and that Lee, lost in his coma, said simply,

"I will give that sum."

He passed a quiet night and died in the morning.

National Archives
General Robert E. Lee's last words, considered not dignified enough for the great warrior, were replaced by fictitious words in his biography.

GEORGE GORDON MEADE

General USA

Philadelphia, Pennsylvania, November 6, 1872

The former commander of the Army of the Potomac commanded various military departments until his death.

"I am about crossing a beautiful wide river, and the opposite shore is coming nearer and nearer."

National Archives
George Meade's last words are strangely similar to those of Stonewall Jackson.

National Archives
George McClellan misunderstood his strength when commanding and when dying.

GEORGE BRINTON McCLELLAN

General USA

Orange, New Jersey, October 29, 1885

McClellan was nominated for the Presidency by the Democratic Party but he was defeated by Lincoln in 1864. From 1878 to 1881 he served as governor of New Jersey. Just before death took him, wishing to send a message to his wife, he said,

"Tell her I am better now."

ULYSSES SIMPSON GRANT

General, USA

Mount McGregor, July 23, 1885

After serving as President of the United States, Grant completed his very successful autobiography despite the fact that he was suffering from cancer and was being treated with morphine. Two weeks before he died he wrote:

> "I do not sleep although I sometimes doze a little. If up I am talked to and in my efforts to answer cause pain. The fact is I think I am a verb instead of a personal pronoun. A verb is anything that signifies to be; to do; or to suffer. I signify all three."

Shortly before he died, he asked for

"Water."

He died at 8 a.m. in his sleep.

LOUISA MAY ALCOTT

Author

Concord, Massachusetts, March 6, 1888

After serving as a Civil War nurse, Alcott went on to become famous as the author of *Little Women* and 269 other published works including *Hospital Sketches,* based on her civil war experiences. Interested in the rights of women, she was the first woman to vote in Concord. She remained unmarried and died at the age of fifty-five. Near the end she said,

"Is it not meningitis?"

JEFFERSON DAVIS

Former President CSA

New Orleans, Louisiana, December 6, 1889

After being captured by Federal cavalry in May, 1865 and held for two years as a prisoner at Fortress Monroe, Davis was released without being tried. He eventually resided at Beauvoir, an estate near Biloxi, Mississippi where he wrote *The Rise and Fall of the Confederate Government.* While traveling in

November, 1889, he caught a severe cold which developed into acute bronchitis, complicated by malaria. In the home of a New Orleans judge, Davis remained under the care of his wife and two doctors. However, after three weeks he weakened and, near the end, refused medicine, saying,

"Pray, excuse me; I cannot take it."

PHILIPPE RÉGIS DÉNIS de KEREDERN de TROBRIAND

General USA

Bayport, New York, July 15, 1897

French-born de Trobriand served in the Union army from the beginning of the war to the end. Continuing in military service after the war, he also found time to develop his literary talents. In a letter written shortly before he died, the eighty-one year old warrior stated:

> "You will understand, dear Bonnaffon, that in such condition it is out of the question for me to receive any visit, or even to designate any possible time of meeting, as by that time it is as likely that I may be underground as on it. Farewell then or "au revoir," as the case may turn. Anyhow I remain, Yours faithfully,
>
> R. de Trobriand."

National Archives

Professional soldier Philippe de Trobriand survived many battles to die at the age of eighty-one years.

LEWIS "LEW" WALLACE

General USA

Crawfordville, Indiana, February 15, 1905

After the war, Wallace served as the Governor of New Mexico Territory having to meet and deal with the infamous Billy the Kid. Later he was the U. S. minister to Turkey. He also became widely known as an author, his most famous work being *Ben Hur: A Tale of the Christ.* To his wife who was at his bedside when he died, he said,

"We meet in heaven."

National Archives

After a life of adventure and fame, Lew Wallace directed his last words to his wife.

VARINA HOWELL DAVIS

New York, New York, October 16, 1906

After successfully lobbying for the release of her husband after the war, Varina united with Jefferson Davis, former President of the Confederacy, and, aided by friends, spent a quiet life at their Mississippi estate, Beauvoir. She wrote her memoirs and, after her husband's death, moved to New York where she wrote articles. On October 6, returning from a summer in the Adirondacks, she contracted a cold that developed into pneumonia. At the Hotel Majestic, surrounded by family and friends, she continued to weaken. The rector of the Episcopal Church was summoned to minister religious comfort. In her last moments of consciousness she said,

"O Lord, in Thee have I trusted, let me not be confounded."

She slipped into a coma and died at 10:25 p.m., aged eighty years.

CLARA BARTON

Civil War Nurse

Glen Echo, Maryland, April 12, 1912

During the war she volunteered to distribute supplies, then became a nurse to Civil War soldiers. After the war she supervised searches for missing soldiers; later she established hospitals in Europe and organized the American Red Cross. As a relief worker, she aided in time of disaster, including the Galveston hurricaine. Death came at the age of ninety from pneumonia. Bed-ridden, she gave up the ghost after a lifetime of service to others, saying,

"Let me go! Let me go!"

National Archives

After a lifetime of service to others, nurse Clara Barton asked for release.

SILAS WEIR MITCHELL

Physician

Philadelphia, Pennsylvania, January 4,1914

Having served as a surgeon in the Civil War, Mitchell went on to become a pioneer in nervous disorders and the workings of the nervous system. He published many medical and literary works including his autobiography. On his death-bed he became delirious, perhaps thinking he was again in the Civil War.

"That leg must come off—save the leg—lose the life!"

LAST MAN STANDING

Sons of the Union Veterans of the Civil War

Last Civil War Soldier, Albert Woolson,
died at the age of 109 years in 1956.

ALBERT WOOLSON

Drummer Boy, USA

Duluth, Minnesota, August 2, 1956

Last survivor of the Grand Army of the Republic, Woolson, a Civil War drummer-bugler boy, died at the age of 109. He enlisted on October 10, 1864 as a member of Company C, First Minnesota Volunteer Heavy Artillery. Never having participated in any battles, he said that the high point of his army career was his firing a cannon when he was seventeen years old. Three years before he died, he reminisced,

> "The colonel handed me the end of a rope and said: 'When I yell you stand on your toes, open your mouth wide, give a yell yourself and pull the rope.' I yanked the lanyard and the cannon went off and scared me half to death."

He recalled that his services were mainly needed at burials.

> "We went along with a burying detail. Going out we played proper sad music, but coming back we kinda hit it up. Once a woman came onto the road and asked what kind of music that was to bury somebody. I told her that we had taken care of the dead and that now we were cheering up the living."

Woolson, destined to be the last man standing, was part of a drum and bugle corps after the war. His last word on the subject--

> "We played fine lively music. Nothing sad."

BIBLIOGRAPHY/REFERENCE [See Index]

Abernethy, Byron R., ed., *Private Elisha Stockwell, Jr. Sees the Civil War,* Norman, University of Oklahoma Press, 1958. [A1]

Adams, Captain John G. B., *Reminiscences of the Nineteenth Massachusetts Regiment,* Boston, Wright, Potter Printing Company, 1899. [A2]

Alcott, Louisa May, *Hospital Sketches,* edited by Bessie Z. Jones, Cambridge, The Belnap Press of Harvard University Press, 1960. [A3]

Alexander, E. P., *Military Memoirs of a Confederate,* Bloomington, Indiana University Press, 1962. [A4]

Alleman, Tillie, *At Gettysburg, or What A Girl Saw and Heard of the Battle,* New York, W. Lake Borland, 1889. [A5]

Allen, M. B., "Letter, October 12, 1864", University Libraries of Virginia Tech, http://scholar2.lib.vt.edu/mss/hcctrans.htm August, 2000. [A6]

Allen, Thomas B., *The Blue and The Gray,* Washington, The National Geographic Society, 1992. [A7]

Alotta, Robert I., *Civil War Justice,* Shippensburg, White Mane Publishing Company, Inc., 1989. [A8]

Angle, Paul M. and Earl Schenck Miers, *Tragic Years, Volume One,* New York, Simon and Schuster, 1960. [A9]

Armstrong, Warren B., *For Courageous Fighting and Confident Dying,* Lawrence, University Press of Kansas, 1998. [A10]

Army and Navy Journal, Volume 2, p. 245. [A11]

Athearn, Robert G., ed., *Soldier in the West: The Civil War Letters of Alfred Lacey Hough,* Philadelphia, University of Pennsylvania Press, 1957. [A12]

Bailey, Ronald H., et al, *Forward To Richmond,* Alexandria, Time-Life Books, 1983. [B1]

Barnard, John, *Deposition Made April 26, 1886,* National Archives, Washington, D. C. [B2]

Barnes, David M., *The Draft Riots in New York, July, 1863,* New York, Baker & Godwin, 1863. [B3]

Barrett, John G., ed., *Yankee Rebel: The Civil War Journal of Edmund DeWitt Patterson,* Chapel Hill, The University of North Carolina, 1966. [B4]

Barton, O. S., *Three Years with Quantrill,* Norman, University of Oklahoma Press, 1992. [B5]

Baruch, Simon, *Confederate Veteran Magazine,* April, 1914, Vol. XXII, No. 4. [B6]

Battle, J. H., W. H. Perrin and G. C. Kniffin, *Kentucky: A History of the State,* Louisville, F. A. Battey, 1885. [B7]

Bauer, K. Jack, ed., *Soldiering: The Civil War Diary of Rice C. Bull,* San Rafael, Presidio Press, 1977. [B8]

Beatty, John, *Memoirs of a Volunteer,* ed., Harvey S. Ford, New York, W. W. Norton & Company, 1946. [B9]

Becker, Carl M., and Ritchie Thomas, eds., *Hearth and Knapsack: The Ladley Letters, 1857-1880,* Athens, Ohio University Press, 1988. [B10]

Beeson, Mary F., *Autobiography,* University of Kansas, http://raven.cc.ukans.edu/carrie/kancoll/articles/beeson.htm, August, 2000. [B11]

Bennett, Brian A., "The Supreme Event in its Existence", *Gettysburg Magazine,* No. 3, July, 1990. [B12]

Benson, Susan Williams, ed., *Berry Benson's Civil War Book,* Athens, The University of Georgia Press, 1992. [B13]

Berlin, Jean V., ed., *A Confederate Nurse: The Diary of Ada W. Bacot, 1860-1863,* Columbia, The University of South Carolina Press, 1994. [B14]

Boston Herald, Boston, August 15, 1863. [B15]

Boston Herald, Boston, April 25, 1864. [B16]

Boston Herald, Boston, April 27, 1864. [B17]

Boston Journal, Boston, September 1, 1863. [B18]

Boston Saturday Evening Gazette, July 7, 1861. [B19]

Boynton, Charles B., *The History of the Navy During the Rebellion, Volume I,* New York, D. Appleton and Company, 1867. [B20]

Boynton, Charles B., *The History of the Navy During the Rebellion, Volume II,* New York, D. Appleton and Company, 1868. [B21]

Brewster, Charles Harvey, *When This Cruel War Is Over,* edited by David W. Blight, Amherst, The University of Massachusetts Press, 1992. [B22]

Brockett, L. P., *The Camp, The Battle Field and the Hospital,* Philadelphia, National Publishing Company, 1866. [B23]

Brown, Elijah S., "Letter, January 23, 1863", Vermont Historical Society, http://www.state.vt.us/VHS/educate/cwletter/brownlet.htm. July, 2000. [B24]

Brumgardt, John R., ed., *Civil War Nurse: The Diary and Letters of Hannah Ropes,* Knoxville, The University of Tennessee Press, 1980. [B25]

Buckland, Chester A., "Letter, April 5, 1862", Rutherford B. Hayes Library, Fremont, Ohio. [B26]

Catton, Bruce, *The Army of the Potomac: Mr. Lincoln's Army,* New York, Doubleday & Company, Inc., 1962. [C1]

Catton, Bruce, *Glory Road,* New York, The Fairfax Press, 1984. [C2]

Chaitin, Peter M. et al., *The Coastal War,* Alexandria, Time-Life Books, 1984. [C3]

Chamberlain, Joshua, "Through Blood and Fire at Gettysburg", *Gettysburg Magazine,* No. 6, January, 1992. [C4]

Chamberlayne, Ham, *Ham Chamberlayne—Virginian,* Richmond, Press of The Dietz Printing Company, 1932. [C5]

Chelsea Telegraph and Pioneer, Chelsea, Massachusetts, January 4, 1862. [C6]

Chelsea Telegraph and Pioneer, Chelsea, Massachusetts, January 25, 1862. [C7]

Chelsea Telegraph and Pioneer, Chelsea, Massachusetts, October 4, 1862. [C8]

Chelsea Telegraph and Pioneer, Chelsea, Massachusetts, December 27, 1862. [C9]

Chelsea Telegraph and Pioneer, Chelsea, Massachusetts, May 28, 1864. [C10]

Chelsea Telegraph and Pioneer, Chelsea, Massachusetts, December 10, 1864. [C11]

Clark, Champ, *Gettysburg,* Alexandria, Time-Life Books, 1987. [C12]

Clark, L. H., *Military History of Wayne County, N.Y.,* Sodus, Lewis H. Clark, Hulett & Gaylord, 1883. [C13]

Clark, Oliver C., "Letter (for James McChesney), May 21, 1865", Letters of James McChesney, National Archives, Washington, D. C. [C14]

Coffin, Charles Carleton, *The Boys of '61,* Boston, Estes and Lauriat, 1881. [C15]

Conyngham, D. P., *The Irish Brigade and Its Campaigns,* 1867. [C16]

Cordlcy, Richard, *The Lawrence Massacre by a Band of Missouri Ruffians Under Quantrell,* Lawrence, J. S. Broughton, 1865. [C17]

Cordley, Richard, *A History of Lawrence, Kansas,* Lawrence, E. F. Caldwell, 1895. [C18]

Corse, John M., "Letter By John M. Corse", http://members.xoom.com/_XMCM/civilwar/corse.htm, July, 2000. [C19]

Cozzens, Peter, "Hindman's Grand Delusion", *Civil War Times Illustrated,* October, 2000. [C20]

Cramer, Clayton E., ed., *By The Dim and Flaring Lamps: The Civil War Diaries of Samuel McIlvaine,* Monroe, Library Research Associates Inc., 1990. [C21]

Culpepper, Marilyn Mayer, *Trials and Triumphs,* East Lansing, Michigan State University Press, 1991. [C22]

Cutrer, Thomas W., "Scurry, William Read", *The Handbook of Texas Online,* http.//www.tsha.utexas.edu/handbook/online/, November, 2000. [C23]

Dana, Charles A., *Recollections of the Civil War,* New York, D. Appleton and Company, 1898. [D1]

Davis, Burke, *Gray Fox,* New York, Rinehart & Company, Inc., 1956. [D2]

Davis, Burke, *To Appomattox,* New York, Rinehart & Company, Inc., 1959. [D3]

Davis, G. W., "Letter, October 1, 1864", Lewis Leigh Collection, Department of the Army, U. S. Army Military Institute. [D4]

Davis, William C., *The Battle of New Market,* New York, Doubleday & Company, Inc., 1975. [D5]
Davis, William C., *Brother Against Brother,* Alexandria, Time-Life Books, 1983. [D6]
Davis, William C. et al., *First Blood,* Alexandria, Time-Life Books, 1983. [D7]
Day, Philip and Trevor Stevens, "In The Wilderness", A Taste of The Oldliner Magazine, Issue 6, http://website.lineone.net/~bullrun/page3.html, April, 2001. [D8]
Dedham Gazette, Dedham, Massachusetts, August 3, 1861. [D9]
De Forest, John William, *A Volunteer's Adventures,* New Haven, Yale University Press, 1946. [D10]
Dinkins, James, *Personal Recollections and Experiences in the Confederate Army,* Cincinnati, The Robert Clarke Company, 1897. [D11]
Dodd, David O., "Letter, January 8, 1864", http://www.civilwarletters.com/dodd_letter.html, July, 2000. [D12]
Dodd, David O., "Letter, January 8, 1864", http://www.civilwarbuff.org/dodd.html, July, 2000. [D13]
Drivers, Robert, ed., *The Diary of Michael Reid Hanger,* http://jefferson.village.virginia.edu/vshadow2/personal/hanger.html, February, 2001. [D14]
Duran, James C. and Eleanor A., eds., *Soldier of the Cross: The Civil War Diary and Correspondence of Rev. Andrew Jackson Hartsock,* Manhattan, MA/AH Publishing, 1979. [D15]
Eby, Cecil D., Jr., ed., *A Virginia Yankee in the Civil War,* Chapel Hill, The University of North Carolina Press, 1961. [E1]
Editors, *Lee Takes Command,* Alexandria, Time-Life Books, 1984. [E2]
Edmonds, S. Emma E., *Nurse and Spy in the Union Army,* Hartford, W. S. Williams & Company, 1865. [E3]
Ellis, Thomas T., *Leaves From the Diary of an Army Surgeon,* New York, John Bradbarn, 1863. [E4]
Flanagan, James W., "Virginia Yankee at Perryville", *America's Civil War,* Vol. 10, No. 1, March, 1997. [F1]
Foster, John Y., "Four Days at Gettysburg", *Harper's New Monthly Magazine,* Volume 28, Issue 165, February, 1864. [F2]
Gallagher, Gary W., ed., *Fighting for the Confederacy,* Chapel Hill, The University of North Carolina Press, 1989. [G1]
Gates, Arnold, ed., *The Rough Side of War: The Civil War Journal of Chesley A. Mosman,* New York, The Basin Publishing Co., 1987. [G2]
Gilmor, Harry, *Four Years in the Saddle,* New York, Harper & Bros., Publisher, 1866. [G3]
Goldsborough, W. W., *The Maryland Line in the Confederate States Army,* Baltimore, Kelly, Piet & Company, 1869. [G4]
Gordon, John B., *Reminiscences of the Civil War,* New York, Charles Scribner's Sons, 1903. [G5]
Haines, Joe D., Jr., "Eyewitness to War: Dr. Hunter McGuire", *America's Civil War,* Vol. 10, No. 5, November, 1997. [H1]
Hall, James E., *The Diary of A Confederate Soldier,* ed. by Ruth Woods Dayton, Privately Printed, 1961. [H2]
Hammer, Jefferson J., ed., *Frederic Augustus James's Civil War Diary,* Rutherford, Fairleigh Dickinson University Press, 1973. [H3]
Hannaford, Ebeneezer, *The Story of a Regiment: A History of the Campaigns, and Associations in the Field of the Sixth Regiment Ohio Volunteer Infantry,* Cincinnati, 1868. [H4]
Harper's Weekly, "The Execution of Champ Ferguson", Volume IX, Issue 463, November 11, 1865. [H5]
Harper's Weekly, "The Execution of Wirz", Volume IX, Issue 465, November 25, 1865. [H6]

Haskew, Mike, "Valley of the Shadow", *America's Civil War,* Vol. 9, No. 5, November, 1996. [H7]
Hawks, Esther Hill, *A Woman Doctor's Civil War,* Columbia, University of South Carolina Press, 1984. [H8]
Headlee, Terry, "Three Lost Their Heads to Fierce Cannon Fire", *The Herald-Mail,* Hagerstown, Maryland, September 10, 1992. [H9]
Horan, James D., *Mathew Brady: Historian With A Camera,* New York, Bonanza Books, 1955. [H10]
Hosier, Scott, "Savage Skirmish Near Sharpsburg", *America's Civil War,* Vol. 11, No. 4, September, 1998. [H11]
Hosmer, James K., *The Color-Guard: A Corporal's Notes of Military Service in the Nineteenth Army Corps,* Boston, Walker, Wise and Company, 1864. [H12]
Jackson, Donald Dale, et al., *Twenty Million Yankees,* Alexandria, Time-Life Books, 1985. [J1]
Jaynes, Gregory, et al., *The Killing Ground,* Alexandria, Time-Life Books, 1986. [J2]
Johnson, Robert Underwood and Clarence Clough Buel, eds., *Battles and Leaders of the Civil War,* New York, Century Co., 1887. [J3]
Jones, Jenkin Lloyd, *An Artilleryman's Diary,* Wisconsin History Commission, 1914. [J4]
Jones, Paul, *The Irish Brigade,* Washington, Robert B. Luce, Inc., 1969. [J5]
Jorgensen, Jay, "Anderson Attacks the Wheatfield", *Gettysburg Magazine,* No. 14, January, 1996. [J6]
Judkins, William Brock, "Memoir", http://www.mindspring.com/~jcherepy/memoir/judkins.txt, February, 2001. [J7]
Katcher, Philip, *Lethal Glory,* London, Cassel, 1995. [K1]
Kimball, June, "An Incident at Gettysburg", http://www.civilwarathome.com/Gettysburgincident.htm July, 2000. [K2]
Kidd, J. H., *Riding With Custer,* Lincoln, University of Nebraska Press, 1997. [K3]
Kirwan, A. D., ed., *Johnny Green of the Orphan Brigade,* The University of Kentucky Press, 1956. [K4]
Korn, Jerry, *Pursuit To Appomattox,* Alexandria, Time-Life Books, 1987. [K5]
Kunhardt, Dorothy Meserve and Philip B. Kunhardt Jr., *Twenty Days,* New York, Harper & Row, Publishers, 1965. [K6]
Ladd, Asa, "Letter to Wife, Oct. 29, 1864" and "Letter to Father, Oct. 29, 1864", http://homepages.rootsweb.com/~ladd/asa.htm, August, 2000. [L1]
Lane, Mills, ed., *"Dear Mother: Don't grieve about me. If I get killed, I'll only be dead.",* Savannah, The Beehive Press, 1977. [L2]
Langhorne, J. Kent, "Letter, June 1, 1863", VMI Manuscript #361, Virginia Military Institute. [L3]
Leckie, Robert, *None Died In Vain,* New York, HarperCollins Publishers, 1990. [L4]
Le Comte, Edward S., *Dictionary of Last Words,* New York, Philosophical Library, 1955. [L5]
Linderman, Gerald F., *Embattled Courage,* New York, The Free Press, 1987. [L6]
Livermore, Mary A., *My Story of The War,* Hartford, A. D. Worthington and Company, 1889. [L7]
Lockridge, "Memoirs of Captain Samuel Brown Coyner", http://jefferson.village.virginia.edu/vshadow2/personal/coyner.html. [L8]
Longacre, Edward G., ed., *From Antietam to Fort Fisher: The Civil War Letters of Edward King Wightman, 1862-1865,* Rutherford, Fairleigh Dickinson University Press, 1985. [L9]
Longstreet, James, *From Manassas To Appomattox,* Bloomington, Indiana University Press, 1969. [L10]
Lowell Sun, Lowell, Massachusetts, April 18, 1911. [L11]
Lowenfels, Walter, ed., *Walt Whitman's Civil War,* New York, Alfred A. Knopf, 1961. [L12]
Marks, J. J., *The Peninsular Campaign in Virginia,* Philadelphia, J. B Lippincott & Company, 1864. [M1]

Marvel, William, *Andersonville: The Last Depot,* Chapel Hill, The University of North Carolina Press, 1994. [M2]
Massachusetts Weekly Spy, Worchester, December 4, 1861. [M3]
McCordick, David, ed., *The Civil War Letters (1862-1865) of Private Henry Kauffman,* Lewiston, The Edwin Mellen Press, 1991. [M4]
McDonald, Cornelia Peake, *A Woman's Civil War,* Madison, The University of Wisconsin Press, 1992. [M5]
McFeely, William S., *Grant,* New York, W. W. Norton & Company, 1982. [M6]
McKnight, Christopher P. C., "Letter, October 18, 1864", http://www.rootsweb.com/~okgenweb/civilwar/letters/10.htm, July, 2000. [M7]
Menge, W. Springer & J. August Shimrak, editors, *The Civil War Notebook of Daniel Chisholm,* New York, Ballantine Books, 1990. [M8]
Miears, Lorenz A., "Excerpt from Diary", Hagerstown, *The Morning Herald,* September 17, 1987. [M9]
Mohr, James C., ed., *The Cormany Diaries,* Pittsburgh, University of Pittsburgh Press, 1982. [M10]
Montgomery, J. R., "Letter, May 10, 1864", Eleanor S. Brockenbrough Library, The Museum of the Confederacy, Richmond, Virginia. [M11]
Morris, Roy Jr., "From the Editor", *America's Civil War,* Vol. 10, No. 5, Nov., 1997. [M12]
Morrison, J. A., "Letter, Sept. 11th, 1863", *The Civil War Letters of James Morrison,* http://www.snymor.edu/pages/library/local_history/sites/letters/sep-11-63.htmlx, July, 2000. [M13]
Morton, Hayward, "Letter, December 19, 1862", Lewis Leigh Collection, Department of the Army, U. S. Army Military Institute. [M14]
Mumey, Nolie, *Bloody Trails Along the Rio Grande: A day-by-day Diary of Alonzo Ferdinand Ickis,* Denver, The Old West Publishing Company, 1958. [M15]
Nevin, David, et al., *The Road To Shiloh,* Alexandria, Time-Life Books, 1983. [N1]
New York Times, August 2, 1956. [N2]
Norder, Steve, "A Mighty Mean-Fowt Fight", *Civil War Times,* February, 1992. [N3]
Oates, Stephen B., *With Malice Toward None,* New York, Harper & Row, Publishers, 1977. [O1]
Oates, William C., "Gettysburg: The Battle on the Right", *http://www.ehistory.com/uscw/features/regimental/alabama/confederate/15thAlabama/gettysburg.cfm,* April, 2001. [O2]
O'Beirne, Kevin M., "Into the Valley of the Shadow of Death: The Corcoran Legion at Cold Harbor", *North & South,* Volume 3, Number 4, April 2000. [O3]
O'Beirne, Kevin M., "Tragedy at Suffolk: the Corcoran-Kimball Affair", *North & South,* Volume 3, Number 6, August 2000. [O4]
Pardoe, Rosemary, "John A. Oates", *http://www.users.globalnet.co.uk/~pardos/JohnOates.html,* January, 2001. [P1]
Parker, William Harwar, *Recollections of a Naval Officer 1841-1865,* Annapolis, Naval Institute Press, 1985. [P2]
Patterson, Gerald A., "The Death of Iverson's Brigade", *Gettysburg Magazine,* No. 5, July, 1991. [P3]
Pettit, Frederick, "Letter, July 9, 1864", The Frederick Pettit Collection of Civil War Letters, *Civil War Times Illustrated* collection, The United States Army Military History Institute, Carlisle Barracks, Pennsylvania. [P4]
Post, Lydia M., ed., *Soldiers' Letters From Camp, Battle-field and Prison,* New York, Bunce & Huntington, Publishers, 1865. [P5]
Potter, Jerry O., *The Sultana Tragedy,* Gretna, Pelican Publishing Company, 1997. [P6]
Pratt, Fletcher, *Civil War in Pictures,* New York, Garden City Books, 1955. [P7]
Read, Emily Hazen, *Life of A. P. Dostie,* New York, W. P. Tomlinson, 1868. [R1]
Redkey, Edwin S., ed., *A Grand Army of Black Men,* Cambridge, Cambridge University Press, 1993. [R2]
Rhodes, Robert Hunt, ed., *All For The Union,* New York, Orion Books, 1991. [R3]

Ricksecker, John, "First Lieutenant Rufus Ricksecker", http://www.iwaynet.net/~1sci/Rufus.htm [R4]

Ricksecker, Rufus, "Letter, September 18, 1864", Rare Books Library, Ohio State University, Columbus. [R5]

Rochester Daily Union and Advertiser, November 18, 1862. [R6]

Rochester Daily Union and Advertiser, June 20, 1863. [R7]

Rosenblatt, Emil and Ruth, ed., *Hard Marching Every Day,* Lawrence, University Press of Kansas, 1992. [R8]

Roxbury City Gazette, Massachusetts, July 11, 1861. [R9]

Roxbury City Gazette, Massachusetts, July 18, 1861. [R10]

Roxbury City Gazette, Massachusetts, September 25, 1862 [R11]

Roxbury City Gazette, Massachusetts, September 3, 1863. [R12]

Scarborough, William Kauffman, ed., *The Diary of Edmund Ruffin, Volume III,* Baton Rouge, Louisiana State University Press, 1972. [S1]

Sears, Stephen W., *Chancellorsville,* Boston, Houghton Mifflin Company, 1996. [S2]

Severance, LaGrange, "Letter, August 1, 1866", http://www.usps.gov/letters/civwar4.html. August, 2000. [S3]

Small, Harold Adams, ed., *The Road to Richmond,* Berkeley, University of California Press, 1939. [S4]

Smith, A. P., *History of the Seventy-Sixth Regiment New York Volunteers,* Cortland, Truair, Smith and Miles, Printers, 1867. [S5]

Spring, Leverett Wilson, *Kansas: The Prelude to the War for the Union,* Boston, Houghton, Mifflin and Company, 1888. [S6]

Stanley, Henry Morton, *The Autobiography of Henry Morton Stanley,* Ed. by Dorothy Stanley, Boston, Houghton Mifflin, 1911. [S7]

Stevens, George T., *Three Years in the Sixth Corps,* Albany, S. R. Gray, Publisher, 1866. [S8]

Stiles, Robert, *Four Years Under Marse Robert,* New York, The Neale Publishing Company, 1903. [S9]

St. Louis Democrat, October 31, 1864. [S10]

Swisher, James K., "Personality: Samuel Garland", *America's Civil War,* May, 1996. [S11]

Sword, Wiley, *Shiloh: Bloody April,* New York, William Morrow & Company, Inc., 1974. [S12]

Thomas, Emory M., *Robert E. Lee: A Biography,* New York, W. W. Norton, 1995. [T1]

Tilley, Nannie M., ed., *Federals on the Frontier: The Diary of Benjamin F. McIntyre 18621864,* Austin, University of Texas Press, 1963. [T2]

Tilly, Kevin, "The Sure-shot 14th Missouri", *America's Civil War,* November 2000. [T3]

Turitz, Leon and Evelyn, *Jews of Early Mississippi,* Jackson, University of Mississippi Press, 1983. [T4]

Underwood, J. J., "Letter, August 29, 1910", http.//www.geocities.com/BourbonStreet/Delta/3843/underwood.htm, October, 2000. [U1]

United States. Naval War Records Office and United States. Office of Naval Records and Library, *Official Records of the Union and Confederate Navies in the War of the Rebellion. /Series I- Volume 7: North Atlantic Blockading Squadron (March 8, 1862 – September 4, 1862),* Washington, Govt. Print. Off., p. 52, 1898. [U2]

United States. Naval War Records Office and United States. Office of Naval Records and Library, *Official Records of the Union and Confederate Navies in the War of the Rebellion. /Series I- Volume 8: North Atlantic Blockading Squadron (September 5, 1862 – May 4, 1863),* Washington, Govt. Print. Off., p. 570, 1899. [U3]

United States. Naval War Records Office and United States. Office of Naval Records and Library, *Official Records of the Union and Confederate Navies in the War of the Rebellion. /Series I- Volume19: West Gulf Blockading Squadron (July 15, 1862 – March 14, 1863),* Washington, Govt. Print. Off., p. 251, 1905. [U4]

United States. War Dept., United States. Record and Pension Office., United States. War Records Office., *et al., The War of the Rebellion: A compilation of the official records of the Union and Confederate armies./ Series 1-Volume 2,* Washington, Govt. Print. Off., 1880. [U5]

United States. War Dept., United States. Record and Pension Office., United States. War Records Office., *et al., The War of the Rebellion: A compilation of the official records of the Union and Confederate armies./ Series 1-Volume 5,* Washington, Govt. Print. Off., p. 328, 1881. [U6]

United States. War Dept., United States. Record and Pension Office., United States. War Records Office., *et al., The War of the Rebellion: A compilation of the official records of the Union and Confederate armies./ Series 1-Volume 11 (Part I),* Washington, Govt. Print. Off., pp. 732-33, 1884. [U7]

United States. War Dept., United States. Record and Pension Office., United States. War Records Office., *et al., The War of the Rebellion: A compilation of the official records of the Union and Confederate armies./ Series 1-Volume 11 (Part II),* Washington, Govt. Print. Off., p. 408, 1884. [U8]

United States. War Dept., United States. Record and Pension Office., United States. War Records Office., *et al., The War of the Rebellion: A compilation of the official records of the Union and Confederate armies./ Series 1-Volume 16 (Part I),* Washington, Govt. Print. Off., p. 758, 1886. [U9]

United States. War Dept., United States. Record and Pension Office., United States. War Records Office., *et al., The War of the Rebellion: A compilation of the official records of the Union and Confederate armies./ Series 1-Volume 17 (Part I),* Washington, Govt. Print. Off., p. 256, 1886. [U10]

United States. War Dept., United States. Record and Pension Office., United States. War Records Office., *et al., The War of the Rebellion: A compilation of the official records of the Union and Confederate armies./ Series 1-Volume 19 (Part I),* Washington, Govt. Print. Off., p. 700, 1887. [U11]

United States. War Dept., United States. Record and Pension Office., United States. War Records Office., *et al., The War of the Rebellion: A compilation of the official records of the Union and Confederate armies./ Series 1-Volume 23 (Part I),* Washington, Govt. Print. Off., p. 497, 1889. [U12]

United States. War Dept., United States. Record and Pension Office., United States. War Records Office., *et al., The War of the Rebellion: A compilation of the official records of the Union and Confederate armies./ Series 1-Volume 30 (Part I),* Washington, Govt. Print. Off., p. 544, 1890. [U13]

United States. War Dept., United States. Record and Pension Office., United States. War Records Office., *et al., The War of the Rebellion: A compilation of the official records of the Union and Confederate armies./ Series 1-Volume 30 (Part II),* Washington, Govt. Print. Off., p. 79, 1890. [U14]

United States. War Dept., United States. Record and Pension Office., United States. War Records Office., *et al., The War of the Rebellion: A compilation of the official records of the Union and Confederate armies./ Series 1-Volume 38 (Part I),* Washington, Govt. Print. Off., p. 813, 1891. [U15]

United States. War Dept., United States. Record and Pension Office., United States. War Records Office., *et al., The War of the Rebellion: A compilation of the official records of the Union and Confederate armies./ Series 1-Volume 38 (Part III),* Washington, Govt. Print. Off., p. 345, 1891. [U16]

United States. War Dept., United States. Record and Pension Office., United States. War Records Office., *et al., The War of the Rebellion: A compilation of the official records of the Union and Confederate armies./ Series 1-Volume 43 (Part I),* Washington, Govt. Print. Off., p. 534, 1892. [U17]

United States. War Dept., United States. Record and Pension Office., United States. War Records Office., *et al., The War of the Rebellion: A compilation of the official records of the Union and Confederate armies./ Series 1-Volume 43 (Part I),*

Washington, Govt. Print. Off., pp. 732-33, 1893. [U18]

United States. War Dept., United States. Record and Pension Office., United States. War Records Office., *et al., The War of the Rebellion: A compilation of the official records of the Union and Confederate armies./ Series 1-Volume 48 (Part I),* Washington, Govt. Print. Off., p. 1185, 1896. [U19]

Voorhees, Alfred H., *The Andersonville Prison Diary of Alfred H. Voorhees,* http://www.snymor.edu/pages/library/local_history/sites/letters/diary.htmlx, July, 2000. [V1]

Wainwright, Colonel Charles S., *A Diary of Battle,* Allan Nevins, ed., New York, Harcourt, Brace & World, Inc., 1962. [W1]

Walker, Charles D., *Memorial, Virginia Military Institute,* 1875. [W2]

Ward, W. C., "Incidents and Personal Experiences on the Battlefield of Gettysburg", *Confederate Veteran Magazine,* August, 1900. [W3]

Watkins, Sam, *Company Aytch,* ed. by M. Thomas Inge, New York, Plume, Penguin Putnam Inc., 1999. [W4]

Waugh, William Archibald, "Reminiscences of the Rebellion", 1908, http.//www.pompano.net/~rwaugh/CivilWar.htm, October, 2000. [W5]

Weathered, John, "The Wartime Diary of John Weathered, 1863", http://userweb.nashville.com/~jack.masters/we1863.htm. July, 2000. [W6]

Wellman, Manly Wade, *Rebel Boast: First at Bethel—Last At Appomattox,* Westport, Greenwood Press, Publishers, 1974. [W7]

Wheeler, Richard, *Voices of the Civil War,* New York, Thomas Y. Crowell Company, 1976. [W8]

Wheeler, Richard, *Witness to Appomattox,* New York, Harper & Row, Publishers, 1989. [W9]

Williams, Scott K., *The Camp Jackson Invasion/ Massacre,* http://www.geocities.com/~sterlingprice/campjackson.htm, February, 2001. [W10]

Winther, Oscar Osburn, ed., *With Sherman to the Sea: The Civil War Letters Diaries & Reminiscences of Theodore F. Upson,* Baton Rouge, Louisiana State University Press, 1943. [W11]

Whitman, Walt, *The Wound Dresser,* Boston, Small, Maynard & Company, 1898. [W12]

Wolcott, Walter, *The Military History of Yates County,* Penn Yan, Express Book and Job Printing House, 1895, p. 103. [W13]

Woolsey, Jane Stuart, *Hospital Days,* New York, D. Van Nostrand, 1868. [W14]

Worchester Aegis and Transcript, Worchester, Massachusetts, June 4, 1864. [W15]

Younce, W. H., *The Adventures of a Conscript,* Cincinnati, The Editor Publishing Company, 1899. [Y1]

INDEX [Refer to Bibliography]